SETTING UP YOUR HOME WORKSHOP

SETTING UP YOUR HOME WORKSHOP

STAN BRAY

ARGUS BOOKS

Argus Books Limited,
1 Golden Square,
London W1R 3AB,
England

ISBN 0 85242 909 6

Typeset by Alan Sutton Publishing Ltd, Gloucester
Printed and bound by L R Printing Services Ltd,
Manor Royal, Crawley, West Sussex, RH10 2QN, England

CONTENTS

INTRODUCTION

My dictionary describes a workshop as "A shop or building where a craft or trade is carried out", but I feel that for the person considering a home workshop the word has much wider implications than this.

As long as I can remember I have had some place or another to carry on with my hobbies. It started as a corner of a table, and then I used a cupboard. There has been a space in a loft, a spare piece of a garage and specially-built buildings. Every time there has been need for a change, through moving home or some similar reason, I have made sure that I profited by my mistakes as well as those of other people. Equally I know that others have profited from my experiences. I have still not yet achieved the perfect workshop and doubt that I ever will. However, as I have progressed so things have improved.

What improvements are we looking for? Many things really: comfort, space, convenience, and something that cannot be described but which undoubtedly contributes to making that workshop your own personal little den.

Frequently when I talk to people who know that I have a workshop I hear the cry. "If only I had one, think what I could do." They go on to think about what they would like to use if for, and there are certainly many hobbies that can be carried on if one has a mind to do so. Usually the reason given for not having their own workshop is lack of space or time. Occasionally it is lack of cash.

None of these is usually a valid reason if one is determined enough. I have already said that I feel the dictionary definition needs widening and so it does. If we make it a *place* where one can carry on a craft or trade then we have widened it to a point where nobody that wants their own workshop need be without one. Notice I now include in the definition space, rather than a building. True, to a large degree this book will be concerned with buildings, but I do not propose to forget those who for various reasons cannot possibly have one.

Many very fine models are constructed without the use of a special building. I know of many modellers who use only a table corner and yet make excellent models. This also applies to craft work such as jewellery making. So we can begin to see that it is highly probable that our workshop will have humble beginnings, and that it can be achieved even if there is no spare space where we live. Taking this a little further before going on to other things, I have many times come across people who are keen modellers and yet who spend all their days travelling the world in the course of their work. Some of them take little boxes with them containing all the essentials they need to make models in their hotel rooms. Just another point to show that premises are not entirely essential.

The above paragraphs certainly do not mean that a good permanent workshop is not desirable. It is, but that building if well laid out need not be very large at all. Throughout this book there will be descriptions of various people's workshops, and the reader will see how some make do with very little space, while others of course have quite large premises. Certainly some sort of permanent place in which to work is a help. It may be necessary to share that space with some other part of the domestic scene but that should not really matter. Over the years I have made model aircraft, boats, small gauge railways, large passenger hauling locomotives, stationary engines and tools, mainly in that order, but there has been some overlapping. The workshop has been continually adjusted to cope with my current interest.

Stocking up with tools can be an expensive business. If we rush out and buy everything we think we are likely to need straight away the bank manager will probably be sending a letter a few days later. Not only that but you will possibly find that many of the things you bought will never be used. The answer is to get things as you go along, and to keep an eye out to see what can be bought second-hand if cash is tight. My own collection of tools has largely been built up over the years by making suggestions when birthdays etc come round. People are always wondering what to buy instead of socks etc and a few loud hints some months earlier works wonders. Another area from which many of my tools have come is the government surplus market. True, this is not as big as it was but it is still there and a means of buying cheap tools. Auctions too can be a good place to buy not only larger equipment but also smaller tools as well.

During one period of my modelling I built "00" gauge locomotives. I cut up tin cans with an old pair of scissors and used a piece of wood with screws through to act as a vice. The models I made were not good, particularly by modern standards, but they pleased me and that is the only thing that counts. I still have them and would not part with them. Gradually things progressed. A cheap vice, the odd file and hacksaw all helped. I still have some of my first tools, even though they are fifty years old. They do not wear out and this is why over the years a workshop is less expensive than we might think.

Of course when eventually I acquired my first lathe more advanced models could be made. The lathe was very small, though, and a few years later I was able to sell it and buy a bigger one. The lathe I sold is still in use after all these years; the one I bought, a Myford ML7, cost me £38 and is still as good today as it was when purchased. It certainly has not worked out expensive by any means!

What I am really trying to say is that to start a home workshop you do not need a miniature factory. In fact very little is needed. If eventually a lathe is purchased then other machines can be built. One thing though is essential, and that is a determination to have a workshop or working space. If the determination is not there then it will never happen. It is no good just to think to oneself wouldn't it be nice to do a thing. It has got to be done. I do hope, though, that those who read this book will be able to save themselves some heartaches by profiting from my and others' mistakes. No one can tell a person how to make his or her workshop: that is something entirely individual, but it does help to be able to follow the advice of others. The book should be read as a whole and not as isolated passages or chapters, the reasons for this being that the advice given and photographs shown in some chapters are equally relevant to others.

Finally I would like to thank all those who helped me write this book – the long-suffering modellers who allowed me to interrupt their activities while I took photographs, and the various manufacturers and dealers who kindly supplied me with, and gave me permission to pass on, information about their products. Without the help of these people I could not have written the book.

1   *MAKING A START*

No Fixed Abode

Although this is a book about setting up and equipping a workshop, let us start by discussing those unfortunates who are for one reason or another unable to have a permanent place in which to work. My own modelling started in this way and I built small model locomotives and model aircraft on the kitchen table.

Assuming we can use a table when it is free from other household duties then all we will need is a tool box in which to keep our tools tidy and a vice with some means of fixing it to the table. There are plenty of vices available for this purpose with clamps on the bottom, or some with suction pads. With the vice in position we are ready to go. If a small lathe can also be available then that is an added bonus and we need nothing more.

The only difficulty with this arrangement is the mess and possible damage that might be caused. If next we acquire a piece of flat board and put this on the table and work on it then the domestic authorities will take a much kindlier view of our activities and so everyone is happier. A piece of wood to screw the little lathe on will also improve things and prevent swarf from falling directly on to the table.

It is now only a short step to put wooden strips along three edges of our wooden base and we are making a considerable improvement as now there is no danger of dirt being pushed over the sides of the board. Incidentally, probably the best material for this board is melamine-faced chipboard. This has a tough facing on it, it cleans easily and is nice and flat.

From the three sides we can progress to four with the fourth one being made removable for working periods. Then if we add a lid we have a box in which, when the side and top are removed, we can work. When fully assembled it will hold our tools. We really have a workshop. True, it must be removed from the table after use, but it is nevertheless self-contained and providing we are not aiming at making very large models it will do all we ask of it.

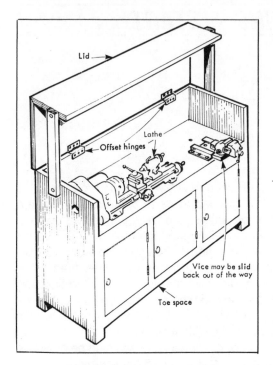

A self-contained workshop unit like this is the ideal answer for those who are forced to work in a kitchen or bedroom where equipment cannot be left out.

So far so good. All that we need now, if we can find a tiny bit of room, is to put four pieces of wood on it to act as legs and we really do have a permanent workshop. It has to be closed down when finished, and may need to be made to match the domestic surroundings, but nevertheless it is a permanent place in which to work and that is what we are after. Our model can remain in position after work. The tools can be put away and when the lid is closed no one would ever know what is in the unit.

Of course with such a unit places can be made to hold tools and so there is really little difference from having one's own room in which to work. Come to think of it, many workshops will need to be shared with garden tools or the car and in many ways, providing the modelling is not going to be on a large scale, the indoor unit is much better.

What I have just described of course is the growth of a mini-workshop. All workshops grow in this way and so it is a general pattern that will be followed.

It is not by any means necessary to stick exactly to the formula given, for it may be possible to adapt the work surface to fit into any convenient nook in the house. It is a principle to think about, and a study of your own particular premises will possibly show just the odd corner that can be utilised in this sort of way.

How Much Space?

The question I am always asked when talking about the subject of setting up a home workshop is "How much space do I need?" and it is not really possible to give an answer to this. It will depend on so many different factors, such as what you want to use the workshop for, how much space you have available and what you can afford to spend. I do know one thing, though, and that is the fact that a great many modellers have managed to make do with very little space indeed and still turn out fine models. Read the story of John Wilks at the end of the book. Although John has now a very large workshop it was not always so. Jeff Stocking, who lives near me, builds large boats in a tiny space. Another that springs to mind is Barry Walls, who is well known as a particularly fine modeller of 0 gauge locomotives for which he has won many prizes. For many years Barry lived in a tiny cottage and the only room it was possible for him to have was a cupboard some two feet by three feet.

Another example is the late Ron Warboys. Ron built absolutely hundreds of locomotives in everything from 00 to 5 in. gauge. He worked in a corner of a kitchen. The supreme example was probably Francois Laluque, who lived in a flat in Paris many floors up. He had a sort of cupboard about five feet long and three feet wide and in this was his bench and lathe. He built 5 in. gauge model locomotives. It was not possible to have the locomotive and himself in the workshop at the same time and so he built a stand on wheels. When the workshop was wanted the locomotive would be wheeled into the hallway where bits would be fitted on as required after making them in the workshop.

So, you see, even if there is not a lot of space there is still no reason why you should not have a workshop. There is something to be said for the smaller sizes as they are easier to heat in the winter. Although my workshops have gradually increased in size over the years I made a Simplex 5 in. gauge model locomotive in a shed seven feet by five and it caused no great problems.

The secret is in the planning of the interior and that we will come to later on. In the meantime I think that most workshops are probably about ten feet by eight but believe me there are very many that are nowhere near as big as that. The bigger the workshop of course the more it will cost to both build and equip, so when you start planning don't go mad and overdo it. At the same time try and plan for the future so that you are not constantly moving from one location to another.

Planning Permission

One of the questions that will enter most minds when thinking about setting up a workshop will be "Do I need anyone's permission?" Before we go into that it is worth thinking about those we know who already have home workshops, and it is probably fair to say that if an honest survey could be made, ninety percent or more have never had any planning permission (except possibly that of the wife or other domestic authority) and nobody gives a hoot about it as long as the owner of that workshop does not inerfere with other people. Thus we prove the saying that the Englishman's home is his castle. But should those people have obtained permission? That is something else entirely and will depend on the circumstances and where the workshop is situated. If the accommodation is rented then there is no doubt that, strictly speaking, the landlord should be approached and the case put to him or her that no harm will be done and so why shouldn't you set up a home workshop? If you own your own house then there are factors that must be taken into account before going ahead.

Under the Town and Country Planning Acts planning permission is required for any alteration of existing use of a building. What does that mean? It means that providing no alteration is made to the actual building nobody will worry if the spare room is converted into a workshop, providing it is not for business purposes. The situation would be that the house is still used as a dwelling and no material alteration has been made to its use. If, however, you get carried away and convert the whole house into a workshop and live somewhere else, or in a tent or caravan in the garden, then that is a different matter. There has then been a material alteration in the use of the house, which has ceased to be a dwelling, and planning permission would most certainly be required. Being more realistic, if in order to get extra light you put an extra window in the room used for the workshop then planning permission may be needed because there will be a structural alteration.

Suppose you decide to use the garage for the workshop and to keep the car in there as well. There should be no problem, the garage is still used as such and the fact that you use it for pleasure as well is of no real interest to the authorities. If, however, you remove the garage doors and brick up most of the front leaving just a single personal type of door then permission may well be required. The same would apply to a loft. Strengthen the beams, lay a chipboard floor and put in a ladder. Nip up and down with your 7¼ in. gauge locomotives and the only one that will worry will be you. Put in a proper staircase and a window and planning permission will be required.

So much, then, for using the existing rooms etc. Suppose we decide to extend the house or garage? Permission is not required providing the volume of the extension does not exceed 50 cubic metres or one tenth of the volume of the house up to a hundred and fifteen cubic metres, whichever is the greater. This is the total area of extension allowed without permission and so if other extensions have been made previously, even though the present one falls within those limits planning permission will be needed. Any such extension must not extend beyond the building line, which is usually the front or side of the house but may in the case of a row of houses be the most forward point of these. If an extension to the house is being made it must not exceed the height of the existing building.

While a permanent place to work is desirable it is not entirely necessary. Each year at Primrose Valley during the modelling week a temporary workshop is set up in an hour or two. The use of small portable lathes and drilling machines plus clamp-on vices enables quite a comprehensive set-up to be organised.

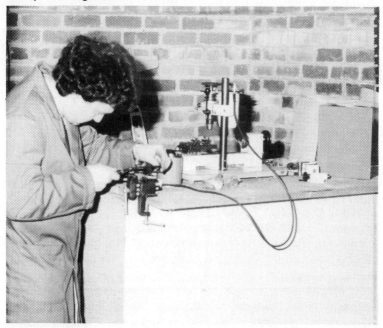

As far as a garden workshop is concerned you are allowed to erect a shed, summer house, greenhouse, pigeon loft, dog kennel etc as long as the total area of the buildings does not cover more than half of the garden. The building must not protrude in front of the house and must not be over 3 metres in height unless it has a ridged roof, in which case the height may be 4 metres. It begins to seem as though officialdom is saying keep it in your own backyard and we could not care less. There can be a proviso to this, though, and that is that the deeds of some houses have a restriction written into them as to what can or cannot be erected in the back garden, my own house is limited to one shed and one greenhouse of specified sizes. This is for reasons of conservation. Conservation may also come into matters if trees are to be cut down, or if the building in which you live is a listed building of historical interest.

There is another set of regulations relating to extending a house or indeed, in theory at least, to putting up a building in a garden. These are the local building regulations, and they differ from authority to authority. While at first one might bristle with indignation at the thought that all building work must be carried out in a certain way, when these regulations are looked at they really are to our own advantage. They are there for our own protection and to prevent annoyance to others.

The regulations relate to structural matters and this is why they differ from area to area. The footings or foundations for our workshop in one district might be adequate at nine inches. In another area the subsoil could be such that footings would never support the building. The regulations are set in such a way that if they are complied with there should be no problems with subsidence or anything else that mother nature might try and throw at us. With this in mind a particular roof structure might not be permissible in one area while it is elsewhere. The regulations also take in to account the needs of your neighbours and prevent the building from causing a nuisance to them.

There may be special provisions if your workshop is to be attached to a house. For example when a garage is attached to a house and a door is made giving direct access from that garage to the house, then the door will almost certainly have to be self-closing and fire-proof for a certain period of time. This is logical: the self-closing part both helps prevent the spread of fire and also prevents fumes from the car entering the house more than necessary. The fire-proof regulation needs no explanation. This all sounds complicated but it is not really so. A simple closing device is easy to fit. If there is glass in the door it will have to be of the type with a wire mesh in it and the door surface will need to be something that will not be too easily combustable. But, as can be seen, the regulations are for the householder's own protection.

Planning permission, whether under the Town and Country Planning Act or the Local Building Regulations, is not as hard to obtain as one might think. Local councillors do not usually prevent people enjoying themselves in their own homes just for the sake of it and if the application is reasonable it will receive favourable acceptance. If for any reason permission is refused under the building regulations the applicant has a right to go to the local magistrates and put the case before them.

The local council Building Inspector is usually only too willing to offer advice on the planning question and contacting him will solve most problems, including how to go about things. His department will have detailed knowledge of both acts and of any relating to conservation in the area. It is better to get such expert advice than to wade through the regulations yourself and possibly get things wrong. Before permission is granted a plan of the house showing where the alterations or extensions are to be made, and a plan of the local area giving details of your property in relation to other properties in the area will be needed. These do not have to be drawn up by an architect, but must be clear, and the one of the house should be to scale. The one for the local area can be obtained from the local council and your own property marked in with a coloured ink. For permission under the building regulations a plan must be drawn of the new workshop giving measurements, and constructional details, such as make-up of floor, walls and roof, and position of windows and doors. If a sectional building is to be used then the suppliers will usually have plans suitable for submission to the local authority which they will gladly give you.

Of course it is quite possible that a workshop can be erected without getting any permission from the local authority even though it should be obtained. It is quite possible that no one would bother about it and that would be that. The local council can order it to be pulled down, though, if they find out about and it does not conform to the law. There is also someone else to be considered and that is the insurance company. If any extension is added they must be notified and it is just possible that they might ask whether permission has been obtained for it. It is then better to be safe than sorry and make enquiries from the local council before going ahead. They will not stop the construction of a workshop for pleasurable purposes just for the sake of it!

2   WHERE?

The Loft

The loft is a space that more often than not is serving only to store unwanted household items. With a bit of thought and some work it can make an ideal place for carrying on a hobby. This can include a home workshop. Whatever we are going to do with our loft it is most probable that some work will be required to make it suit the purpose for which we need it, the first obvious thing being if possible the fitting of a loft ladder. These come in various shapes and sizes and if possible one that is nice and solid should be used. I say 'if possible' as loft ladders require a certain amount of clearance between them and the roof and also between them and a wall if there is one nearby. They work on the principle of folding up as the trap door is closed, but as they only fold at the most to two or three pieces it will be seen that even when closed the sections are still quite long.

There is a type of loft ladder that works in a concertina fashion and this will require virtually no clearance at all. However, because of its very nature, while of adequate strength it is somewhat flimsy and when in use is not as rigid as the heavier ones. It will still serve the purpose, though, and so do not despair of using a loft just because the clearance is not as good as you would wish.

The structure of the loft itself will need to be looked at, as many of the modern ones are rather lightweight. Most houses built before, say, 1920 will have very heavy rafters and joists and these will easily take any weight that is going to be put on them. After that period, and particularly post-1950, building methods changed and the timber used became much thinner. To offset this a different type of structure was used and it may be that some slight alterations will be needed before use can be made of the space.

The first thing to be looked at is the joists on which our floor will be put. If these are of timber less than eight inches by two inches in size then the flooring area to be used should be supported by further joists laid over the top of the existing ones. They need to be laid in such a manner that the load is spread beyond the area used as a workshop and indeed if possible so that they obtain the support of the house walls when possible. These new joists should be eighteen inches or ½ metre apart and the timber used should be or 100mm × 50mm section. On top of this should be laid either flooring boards of at least 20mm thickness or flooring quality chipboard. Unfortunately because the opening is quite small the chipboard will have to be cut into strips to get it into the loft. It must then be laid so that the joins along the strips go in the right-angle direction to the joists. Any joins on the length of the strips of chipboard should be made to meet on a joist.

It will be necessary to line the rafters with some material to act as walls and possibly a ceiling as well. Insulation board is ideal for this and it can be laid directly on to the rafters. Between the rafters where it is laid should be insulated with Rockwool, fibreglass or some similar material. Although the loft is within the house it will get very hot in summer and extremely cold in winter unless there is adequate insulation.

The loft is usually a very easy place from which to pick up an electricity supply as most of the house supply runs through it and there should be lots of junction boxes to pick up from. The lighting supply should be taken off separately from the power. Both should run into the workshop area and re-located via a consumer unit so that they are separately fused, from each other and the household supply. When leaving the workshop the supply should be switched off at these units. Places where sockets are to be located will need strengthening with wooden battens on which to fix the

TYPICAL LOFT CONSTRUCTION   SUGGESTED ALTERATIONS

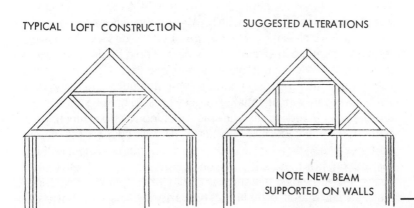

NOTE NEW BEAM
SUPPORTED ON WALLS

Three light lathes, the Unimat 1 (converted to a jig saw) and the Unimat 3 (with milling and drilling attachment) plus the all-plastic Playmat, capable of quite useful work, all highly suitable for a loft workshop. With a suitably strengthened floor heavier machines are quite practical.

electrical equipment. These battens should be fixed securely to the rafters or uprights which support the workshop walls.

There are refinements that can be made, such as putting in a window and enlarging the hatch that gives access to the loft. In some larger houses there may even be room to put a permanent staircase to the loft. This, if done properly, will enhance the building and raise its value. Putting in a larger opening needs some thought. The builder would have calculated the size of opening required for strength and no doubt it will have meant a joist being parted at some point. We cannot afford to have too many joists dealt with in this way for obvious reasons. If possible then any increase in size of the opening should be done in such a way that the extension goes along the joist that is already parted rather than cutting through another one. It is quite surprising how even six or eight inches makes a difference in gaining access, so there is no need to extend the opening by too much. If a permanent staircase is being fitted this will support the rafters from below and so a larger opening can be made. We get nothing for nothing, however, and it will be necessary to support the joists of the floor on which the staircase will stand. This is a comparatively simple matter of bolting timbers to the joists in that area, once more to spread the load.

Putting a window in the loft is a little trickier. First of all it is most probable that planning permission will be required. Then comes the question of what sort of window. The dormer type is possibly the best, but this will involve cutting through rafters and they must be supported while the work is carried out. The top and bottom of where the cuts are to be made will need this support. The window frame can be of wood and once in position, if properly joined to the rafters that have been cut, will provide them with support. If you are making a dormer window try and make it so that it fits exactly between rafters and gives support in that way.

The top or roof of the dormer window should have a slight slope on it to allow rain to run off. The roof can be dealt with as explained elsewhere as far as covering is concerned. The sides of the dormer can be dealt with in a variety of ways, the choice being wood, tiles or felting. Do not forget the necessity for rain strips on the window itself.

The other type of window is the skylight. This is a flat window laid on the slope of the roof. It can be built up using 200mm × 50mm timber and the glass fitted to it in a frame. Either felt or zinc flashing must be fitted right round the window and under the roof tiles at the high point. On the sloping section and the low point it can be laid on the outside of the tiles. This type of window looks easy to make but in fact is remarkably difficult as when the rain runs down the roof in a heavy storm it tends to ride over the frame and if it is possible to get in it will find a way.

It is also possible to lay in a skylight by fitting a section of glass in place of, say, four roof tiles. This is a case of removing the tiles and laying the glass underneath. Lightweight glass should not be used under any circumstances for this purpose – if possible it should be plate glass. These days the edges can be sealed with one of the proprietary sealers which saves much time and trouble. Previously some fairly intricate flashing arrangements were required. Fortunately with the modern sealing compounds it is possible to work from the inside and avoid the need to clamber on to the roof.

A loft then will make a good workshop. It can be fitted out in the normal way. Most workshops in the loft will be used, one suspects, for smaller modelling projects. Unless a permanent staircase has been made it is hard to imagine dragging large lathes and milling machines up into a loft. Quite a nice workshop can be organised using the smaller machines that are available and these will help to make very good models indeed. We are certainly looking at a capability of making 3½ in. gauge locomotives and 1 inch scale traction engines, plus of course stationary engines, clocks etc. A properly designed workshop in the loft can be self-contained and warm and cosy and the area is well worth thinking about, especially for those with no other available space. Noise may be a slight problem and so machines should be mounted on foam rubber to cut this down. Some form of carpet laid on the floor with if possible a foam rubber underlay will also help. That apart there is absolutely no problem whatever.

The Garage

For those who have garages here is a fairly obvious place in which to build a workshop. A lot will depend on the size of the garage and how much space is left once the car is in it or indeed if one is willing to leave the car to the elements and take the garage over entirely as a workshop.

Let us start with the assumption that there is not a great deal of room and that we do not wish the car to be left out. In this case the workshop will have to be something of a compromise and care taken that everything can go away when we have finished with it. Tools will need to be stored in cupboards kept on the walls probably above the height of the car roof, and the lathe will have to be fitted on a narrow bench, unless you are going to stick to the smaller type of lathe and put it away in a cupboard when finished. In either case the lathe and any other machinery will need to be covered when not in use. Cars tend to bring a lot of damp in to the garage and we need to keep this away from the machines if possible. In any case if the car shares the space all tools should be kept well covered with a rust resisting fluid. At one time Ensis oils would have been used. Nowadays we can use one of the proprietary sprays such as WD40 or we can use a product called Duck Oil. All of these fluids have the ability to separate damp from metal and will keep rust off tools. The tools will need to be constantly covered in whatever is used as the application of a coat soon wears off, particularly if the tool is used.

A bench can be made that will fold up against the wall so allowing the driver to get out of the car when putting it away. In most cases where space is as confined as this the car will have to be taken from the garage in order to work at the bench anyway. However, even if there is room to get to a bench and work with the car inside it may be prudent to make the bench so that it folds back against the wall in case at any time there is need of the extra space, for example if work has to be carried out on the car. If we have a slightly larger garage it will be possible to partition it

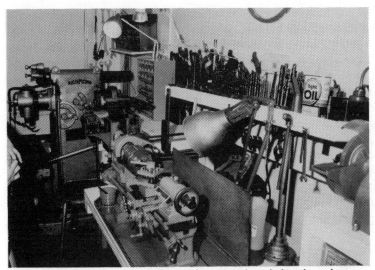

The garage doors on Ted Jolliffe's white-painted workshop have been effectively sealed off to prevent cold from getting in, as can be seen from this photograph.

off so that we can in fact make a workshop inside it. There are a great many workshops like this and it works out well. My own present one uses one end of a double garage. The partitioning need not be all that strong providing the garage can be made secure. We must always think of security and if for any reason the garage cannot be secured then the partitioning will need extra strengthening. For normal purposes a framework of 50mm × 50mm wood covered each side with 12mm chipboard will make a nice partition, and heavy enough on which to hang tools. Do not forget that there should be insulating material between the two layers of chipboard to keep the workshop at a nice temeprature. If chipboard is not fancied then tongued and grooved timber will do as well and in many ways may even be an improvement over chipboard.

It may be a good idea to put a window in the partitioning, and probably a door as well. If the workshop is at the rear of the garage and that is where the garage window is a full wooden partition makes the rest of the garage quite dark. A small window will give enough light to see what you are doing. A door is useful as it saves dashing round the front of the garage if you want anything from there. I find that although I keep all the engineering tools in the workshop I from time to time make use of the car jack or axle stands for supporting things. I have put a door in and go straight in and get what I want. I also find that in fine weather if I leave the garage doors open the window gives me some light in the workshop.

If you are planning to buy a door or use a second-hand one you will probably find that the partitioning will need to be a little stronger than I suggested. It certainly will where the door is hung. For this reason I would suggest making up a lighter door and using this. It can be made so that it can be quite secure. Again if I quote my own experience, I made the door from 30mm × 30mm timber and this proved to be adequate. The bottom part was finished with hardboard and the top has a sheet of plastic in it to allow light through. At my previous workshop this light was not needed and so I made the door with complete hardboard covering. Part of the door where the handle and lock is will need to have extra wood in it to act as support for the lock. One solid piece say 150mm × 30mm will do for this, although I used the 30 × 30 timber and stuck four lengths together.

Some time ago there was an interesting article in *Model Engineer* from someone who was using a garage as a workshop.

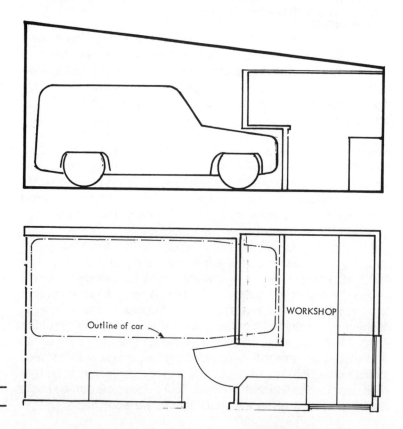

Outline of car

WORKSHOP

There was not quite sufficient room for a full workshop and so he in fact built it in such a way that part of it went over the top of the car bonnet. A very ingenious arrangement and one which would give plenty of added space. It also means that tools can be left in position when not in use.

When a garage is used as a workshop, whether it is shared with a car or not attention must be given to insulating it both on the roof and the walls. If room is really tight the walls may have to be left, although it is hoped not as they can be a cause of condensation and rust. The ceiling and roof *must* be done and how to do this is explained elsewhere.

Another thing that will need attention is the floor. Most garage floors are not fitted with a damp proofing membrane and in wet weather damp will rise up. The floor must therefore be sealed. This can either be done with one of the many proprietary sealers or with a proper paint. Details of floors are dealt with elsewhere and reading that chapter will help the reader to decide the method most suited to him or her.

If the whole garage is in use and it has an up and over door, then this will need some attention, both to make it draught and damp proof and to make it secure. These doors are not difficult to draughtproof: some 25mm × 25mm wood screwed and glued round the top and sides will usually work wonders. Even if the

Although he now has a purpose-built workshop Brent Hudson used a garage for a long while. As he liked building very large models the double doors were a bonus and not dealt with by sealing up as is usual, being necessary for the removal of models.

A bench-top placed over the sink unit is the basis of this simple workshop set up in a touring caravan.

garage is to be partitioned this is a job worth doing as it will prevent cold getting to the workshop shell and so keep it warmer.

Properly organised garages make excellent workshops and are well worth using. There can be some little inconvenience but this is usually a small price to pay for the space available.

Using a Caravan

A caravan can make an excellent little workshop. It is an ideal shape, has plenty of natural light and the walls are insulated. The windows will possibly need some form of double glazing, as caravans suffer very badly from condensation, but the simple way to do this is to put up polythene sheeting.

What, if any, work is carried out on the interior is a matter that will depend on the use to which the van is put apart from its workshop activities. If it is to be used solely as a workshop then the interior can be fitted out permanently as is required. If it is to be used for holidays then obviously the equipment put in it will need to be portable.

In these cases it is usually possible to cover the sink unit with a sheet of chipboard and to mount a non-permanent vice on this. A small lathe and drilling machine can also be put on it. Some plastic sheeting can be used to protect upholstery etc.

I know of two people who have caravans permanently converted for use as workshops and another couple who make use of the van when not using it for touring. It is space that is otherwise unlikely to be used and so well worth thinking about.

Indoor Workshops

The workshop situated inside a house has very many advantages. It is for a start very convenient, as one can pop in any time and not have to face that dark walk in snow or rain that is so often the case with the outside workshop. There is usually less of a heating problem as well, the room being well insulated and frequently centrally heated. The only possible disadvantages are dirt, which will find its way from the workshop into the house, and the possibility of noise. The latter can be considerably reduced as far as machinery is concerned by insulation. Mount the machines on rubber or foam pads and the battle is all but won. If more is needed then a board between the machines and the wall with foam rubber in between should do the trick.

Obviously a downstairs room is the best if it is available, but it has been shown that most home workshops are situated upstairs and so it would seem that many people cope with the situation in spite of any disadvantage there may be. True, noise will be more of a problem upstairs than down but not greatly so. Getting machinery in, if it is required, can be heavy going but it only has to be done once, so again it is nothing much to worry about. Probably the biggest difficulty is for people building large models that have to be kept in the workshop and taken up and downstairs each time they are wanted.

It is possible that the only work that will be required for the indoor workshop, other than fitting out which is dealt with elsewhere, is slightly to strengthen the floor under machinery and possibly under benches. This will not apply downstairs on a concrete floor but certainly will on a wooden one. Nothing much to it really – simply lay a piece of heavy chipboard over the existing floor in such a way that it will spread the load a little. It need not even be fixed down, but just laid there and held in place by the weight on top of it. Another way is to screw wooden bars on the bottom of the legs of benches so that they extend over the ends and just spread the weight instead of putting it all on the points where the legs touch the floor.

It is as well to remember that when you have finished with the room as a workshop the next tenant or owner will probably not want the room used for the same purpose. Care should thus be taken to ensure that walls that are likely to get splashed with oil are covered with some sort of covering that will prevent the oil soaking into the plaster. Once it is there it will not come out again. A good thing to use for this is wall boards. These are thick plywood or hardboard sheets covered with a plastic material, usually in a wood pattern. They look nice and can easily be wiped clean.

Alternatives to this are either to tile vulnerable places or to stick on a wallpaper or similar covering that will be proof against oil. There are plenty of these on the market and a wide choice of colours and patterns. A good floor covering that will protect against oil, such as vinyl, is also desirable if possible, and a mat to wipe swarf etc off your shoes when coming out will maintain domestic harmony.

These few things apart it is mainly a case of just putting in the workshop equipment and making a start, although some adjustment may be needed to electric points and lights so that you do not have wires trailing everywhere.

3   BUILDINGS

Sectionalised Buildings

It is most probable that the majority of home workshops are out of doors in the back garden, either making use of an existing building or one especially erected for the purpose. Let us then assume that we are going to erect a building and see the various ways of going about doing so.

The easiest way by far is to purchase a sectionalised building of which there is a vast range available. These are sold as garden sheds, summerhouses, garages and for all sorts of other reasons but few are actually called workshops. Whichever way the buildings are described, if it is the right size and shape for our purpose, that is all we will need. The buildings, whether of wood or other materials, come in sections and are then bolted together; usually a service is available for this to be done if the purchaser does not want to do it him or herself.

The first thing to do, assuming that planning permission has been granted, is to get hold of some literature and browse through. There will be pictures, which will be either photographs or artist's impressions of the various buildings, but if you read further it will be seen that in fact the panels from which they are made are often manufactured in such a way that the building can be assembled in many ways to fit into the required space. Where this is the case then a form is supplied to enable the right size and shape of building to be ordered, with the doors and windows situated where required. All of which are most useful features.

Once the sizes have been decided on the base can be laid and the building ordered. Laying the base is dealt with elsewhere in this book. The question is what to look for when buying the building. Firstly we must decide, I think, whether the materials are suitable. The vast majority of these structures are made of wood and this can be a very suitable material providing the inside is dealt with correctly and the outside maintained with regular coats of preservative. For general model-making, woodworking etc. the wooden shed is entirely suitable. Should we be planning to use a great deal of heat, for example if we are going to house a small foundry in it, or if we are going to be brazing very large boilers, then it is obviously not the best material and we must look for something else.

When ordering the building we should be looking first of all for the right size and shape, and then for such things as window positioning and doorways. If large models are to be made or bulky machinery taken in and out, the doorway must be as wide as possible. The windows too need to be fairly large to allow in sufficient light, but not so large as to get to the stage where there is not sufficient wall space for our storage units and benches. Neither should windows come down too low. The bottom of the window ideally needs to be just below shoulder height, or even a fraction higher. There is then room to put things underneath, either in the form of benches or storage. An opening window or two is also a desirable feature so that in summer air can be allowed in. If windows can be placed on two or more sides then this can help. As the sun travels round so light will penetrate at various points. With a window on just one wall, there will only be one part of the day when there is full daylight in the building.

Sectional buildings are also available in concrete, steel, and plastic. Providing these are properly insulated then they are very good and will make good workshops. The plastic ones are the least desirable and if a choice is there then I would prefer one of the other materials. Although difficult to insulate, concrete is very strong and requires no maintenance. It is an ideal medium if there is to be a lot of heat involved in the work that will be carried out inside.

When selecting the building a small garage might be worth considering. It has many advantages. More often than not they are available with nice high windows of the type that we will be requiring. The double doors can also be useful. One can be sealed off semi-permanently and used only if it is needed. Alternatively it might well be possible to obtain an extra end with a smaller personal door instead of the wide car entrance type. This is quite feasible with a sectionalised building.

It is possible to obtain a variety of finishes on concrete buildings, and particularly on garages. Many manufacturers make a variety of imitation brick finishes as well as various stone ones. Whilst these will not make the building any better as a workshop it will enhance the appearance and possibly allow it to blend in with existing buildings. After all, we would soom become unpopular

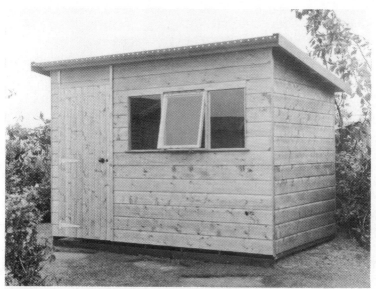

A typical flat or pent roof sectionalised wooden building by Regal Buildings Ltd. The windows are the ideal height for a workshop.

A pointed or apex roofed building by Regal Buildings Ltd. The door can be arranged on these buildings to open left or right handed. Floors can be obtained to fit the buildings but will need some strengthening if machinery is to be installed.

Certainly not designed as a workshop but this summerhouse by Regal Buildings Ltd could have some advantages. The opening windows are a nice height for the purpose and the shutters would help security.

both with our own domestic authorities and with neighbours if the building was to look unsightly.

Build Your Own

By building one's own workshop the desired shape and size can be obtained. It is going to take longer than when purchasing a prefabricated building but many will feel that they are able to get something nearer to their individual requirements by so doing. There is a wider choice available because if desired the building can be constructed of brick as well as of the other materials already suggested.

Let us start with the wooden building. We first of all need to lay our base, of course. The framework can then be made. For this timber of at least 50mm × 50mm section should be used and if possible heavier section, which would give a better result. The framework can be fitted together with simple woodworking joints, or with the special brackets which are now available in several varieties. These save a lot of time and effort. Do not be tempted to make a lot of special wood joints unless you are a master craftsman! Dovetails and the like are not required for this sort of work, it is doubtful if they provide extra strength to the building and

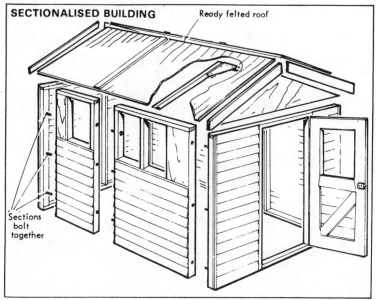

SECTIONALISED BUILDING Ready felted roof

Sections bolt together

If you intend building your own workshop structure the best way is to construct it in sections.

they take a great deal of time. Simple halving joints and possibly a mortise and tenon are all that will be needed.

Do not skimp on the bracing of the building. Uprights should be no more than eighteen inches apart and there should be diagonals to act as braces. These really do strengthen the building

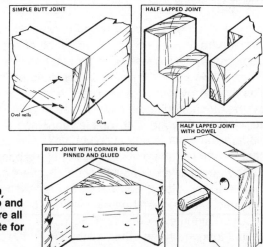

SIMPLE BUTT JOINT

HALF LAPPED JOINT

Oval nails

Glue

HALF LAPPED JOINT WITH DOWEL

BUTT JOINT WITH CORNER BLOCK PINNED AND GLUED

Simple butt, butt with corner block, half tap and half lap with dowel are all simple joints adequate for sectional shed construction.

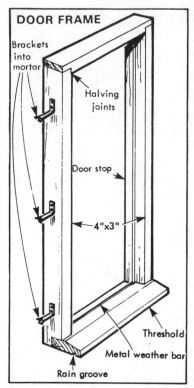

DOOR FRAME

Brackets into mortar

Halving joints

Door stop

4"x3"

Door and window frames need to be substantial. The brackets tie them to brickwork.

Threshold

Metal weather bar

Rain groove

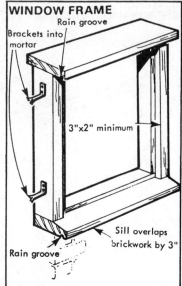

WINDOW FRAME

Rain groove

Brackets into mortar

3"x2" minimum

Sill overlaps brickwork by 3"

Rain groove

SPRAGGED BRACKET

Used for fixing door and window frames, may also be used to join brickwork

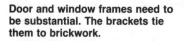

framework no end. Timber round doors and windows which is to form the framework for these should be of heavier section wood. Door and window frames can be purchased if one wishes.

The outside of the building can be covered in a variety of ways. Boards that overlap can be used, and the commonest of these can be purchased in the form of feather edging. The timber is cut thicker at one edge than at the other and this allows for easy overlapping. This is a convenient type of timber for finishing, but after weathering there is a possibility of the boards springing apart slightly and allowing water to get in. A sheet of polythene should therefore be placed between the boarding and the frame. Tongued and grooved boarding is quite popular. In this the board is slotted along one edge and machined to form a corresponding central tongue on the other. When joined the boards form a nice comparatively draught-free finish.

Another possibility is to cover the outside with a marine ply. Slightly more expensive than the other suggestions so far, but a very good finish can be obtained that will withstand the weather and remain proof against the heaviest rains.

The framework can be covered with other material such as corrugated iron sheeting if one so wishes. Some of the various plastic sheetings can also be used, but personally I do not think them very desirable. Whatever the material being laid on the outside of the timber framework it is a very good practice to first of all fix a sheet of polythene over it. This can be done with staples and if you do not have a suitable stapling machine then they can be hired very cheaply indeed. The polythene sheeting ensures that the building remains water and draught proof in even the worst of weathers, and with the material being so cheap to purchase then it is well worth the small cost and little effort involved.

The next possibility open to us is that of brick building. This includes the use of some of the larger building blocks that can be obtained, some with stone faced finishes which may be desirable to match the house. Bricklaying is not that difficult. The bricks are laid in rows on a mortar which is fine sand and cement mixed at a ratio of about seven parts of sand to one of cement. Special mortar cement can be bought which is designed for the purpose, but ordinary cement can be used. When mixing, a platiciser should be included with the water, This is a liquid which keeps the mortar in a nice plastic state while it is being used. If this cannot be bought then use liquid detergent, which will do almost as well.

A layer of mortar is put on the base, say sufficient for about five bricks to be laid on. The bricks are then put on to the mortar and levelled. This can be done by tapping with a hefty piece of wood. Check each one both lengthwise and across with a spirit level to ensure that it is right. For the beginner this is a long job but very rewarding. It is frustrating when watching a professional bricklayer at work and seeing how easily he does the same job. The second layer of bricks is half lapped over to form a bond. Look at any house made of bricks to see how this is done. Do not at this stage worry about getting the mortar between the bricks nice and tidy, as this is done later.

As the brickwork progresses in height a plumb line will have to be used to ensure that the wall is upright. Lines should also be laid to help get the wall straight. It looks easy enough to do and with these guides is, but without them the wall will look like ocean waves. Do not hurry and it is surprising how the technique improves and you become adept at the building. After an hour or so run a trowel round the edges of the mortar to remove any loose bits and then fill in the gaps that are left. The mortar needs to be pushed into the brickwork. This can be done with a piece of plastic piping which will ensure a nice neat finish to your wall. The operation is called pointing and it not only makes the wall look neat but will allow rain to run off. If the pointing is not carried out the wall will become very damp. The mortar used for pointing can also be finished with a trowel, the top edge slightly undercutting the bricks so that the finished mortar is at an angle which allows the water to drain.

In between the second and third layer of brickwork a piece of damp proofing material should be laid to provide a damp course. This prevents the damp from rising up the wall. If the larger building blocks are being used then the damp proofing should be laid on the first course. The door frame should have been put in place and supported before starting bricklaying. The work can then be taken up to the frame. Brackets are put in the frame to fit in between courses of the brickwork and they will eventually secure the frame. The window frames should be laid on the brickwork at the required height, and again as the height of the brickwork progresses the brackets will be covered with mortar and support the frame. When finished the gaps that will inevitably be left between these frames and the bricks can be filled with a proprietary filler, the type squeezed from a tube being the best.

During the work it will be necessary to cut bricks or blocks. This is done by chiselling round the outside to make a deep score right round at the required point and then giving the brick a smart tap, when it should come apart at exactly the point where the scoring took place. A very wide chisel called a bolster is the best tool to use for this.

If the wall is over eight feet in length piers should be made at suitable intervals to act as supports. An unsupported wall is rather vulnerable if this is not done. If the wall is to be joined to an existing building, if possible the brickwork should be keyed into the original wall. To do this remove some bricks from the original wall and insert bricks that will be part of the new wall. Providing the workshop is not too massive this can be got round by screwing angle brackets at frequent intervals to the existing wall, the forked ends of which are held in the mortar of the new one.

The roof can be supported on beams either laid into the brickwork or held with a bracket. This is explained in the chapter dealing with roofs and ceilings. Before fitting the glass in the

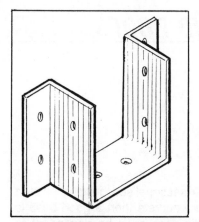 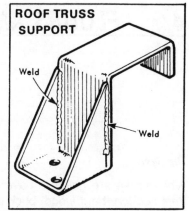

ROOF TRUSS SUPPORT

Weld

Weld

A fabricated roof truss support, left, and a bracket commercially available, for screwing to a wall to support the end of a beam.

windows give the brickwork time to dry out. Should the weather be wet cover the window frames with plastic sheeting to keep the damp out. The door can be dealt with in a similar manner. When building from brick the opportunity should be taken where possible to incorporate any strengthening points that might be needed. For example if the workshop is to be used for heavy constructional or repair work build in a steel joist that can be used to support a hoist of one sort or another.

4   FLOORS AND ROOFS

The Base

Whether we are going to have a sectionalised building or start from scratch, be it wood, brick or concrete then a good base is essential. The depth to which this goes must be dependent to quite a degree on the local soil conditions. In some areas a mere six inches would probably do but in others it may need something like two feet. The local building inspector can advise on this and there will certainly be minimum specifications for wall footings in local regulations. If neighbours have built extensions or garages ask them as they will know what depth they had to go to. It is as well with a workshop to be cautious and to go a little deeper with the foundation as over the years equipment gets added to and before you know where you are there is an awful lot of weight involved. I did not realise quite how much until I moved house on one occasion. I wanted to move the workshop equipment separately and used a three ton van. I had help from some friends but the weight we found was too much for the van to take in one go. This was only metal, a couple of lathes, a drilling machine, a small milling machine and some tools and models. It is really very surprising how it adds up and so you can see why a good base is necessary.

The base will obviously need to be big enough for the building to go on. In the case of prefabricated wooden sheds this should be an inch smaller than the lengths of the sides. So if you have a shed 8 feet by 6 then the base should be 7 feet 11 inches by 5 feet 11 inches. The suppliers will invariably provide you with a suitable plan for the base anyway. For a brick-built construction, and this includes the use of building blocks, then make it some six inches larger each way than what the building is planned to be.

The base will consist of a layer of hardcore covered with a layer of concrete. Hardcore consists of broken bricks, stones etc. It must be hard material, as the name implies, and so do not be tempted to put any ash or other such material in it. We start by digging a hole of suitable depth to take the amount of hardcore required. Remember that the hardcore will really be the thing that is supporting the building, the concrete mainly acting as a sort of mat. When the hole is completed ram the bottom layer of earth down as hard as you can. It should then be left for a while to allow the ground to settle. Don't be in too much of a hurry to start putting in the hardcore. When the ground has settled then the hardcore can go in. Cover the whole thing to about four inches deep and ram the hardcore down hard again. More hard core can be added and rammed in until the hole is about three quarters full.

At this stage wooden planks must be put round and levelled up. This is called shuttering. The wood can be held in position with wooden stakes driven into the ground on the outside. Care must be taken with the levelling as upon this will depend how well the building will stand. The shuttering must be of a width such that it will be level with the top of the concrete when the base is finished. More hardcore can be put in when the shuttering is in position. The base should then be left to settle and again the longer the better. If while it is settling the weather is bad, with snow and frost or even heavy rain, so much the better.

We then come to the concreting and we definitely do not want frost if we can help it while this is being carried out. The concrete will consist of a mix of ballast, which is stones and sand, and some cement. The mixture should be about five shovels of ballast to one of cement if mixing by hand, and seven of ballast to one of cement if a machine is to be used.

To mix it by hand find a nice smooth hard surface somewhere nearby and throw down about fifteen shovels of ballast. Then throw on three of cement making sure you spread it across the ballast. Repeat this about ten times and then carefully mix it all up until it goes a uniform grey colour. Ballast is sold by the cubic metre and you may well need several for the base. If the length times width is multiplied by the depth the amount can easily be calculated. Do not be tempted to try and mix it all at once. Mix it in sections as above and then throw it all together. When it is all done split it into sections so that you have several little mountains about a metre high. Open these out so that they have hollows in them and fill these hollows with water. Allow the water to soak right in and then put in some more. Repeat the operation about three times. Then keep turning each pile over until it is thoroughly mixed. It needs to be about the consistency of a thick cream.

If you do not want to mix the concrete by hand it is possible to hire a mixer that will either work by petrol or electricity. It saves a lot of hard work. With a mixer it is simply a case of putting in seven shovels of ballast and one of cement and so on and then turning it on. When the mix is all right put in the water. Another alternative is to purchase ready-mixed concrete. This will arrive on a predetermined day in a lorry and it can be poured from this. If there is a suitable access it is quite probable that it can be poured direct onto the hardcore. If not it will be left in a suitable place and have to be transported on a wheelbarrow. This can be a somewhat harrowing experience as once the concrete is delivered it needs to be put in and levelled quite quickly as otherwise it will harden before you can get it in. A lump of solid concrete stuck in the drive is no joke!

If you are moving into a new house and the builders are still about it may be possible to get the base laid at a reasonable price by the builders, who will have everything to hand, hardcore, shuttering and concrete. All you do is dig the hole. It may even be possible to get the builders to do this for you.

The concrete needs to be laid to within about three inches of the top of the shuttering, and can then be levelled off with a shovel. When set a damp-proof membrane should be put over the top. This is a posh name for a sheet of plastic material. It should be laid as one sheet if possible, but if it is not possible then there should be an overlap of at least six inches. This is going to prevent damp coming through and if there is not sufficient overlap it might get past.

About 1 × 3in. is minimum size for the plank, used edge-on.

LEVELLING CONCRETE WITH A PLANK, USING SAWING AND TAMPING MOVEMENTS

Note edge strips to maintain correct thickness

More concrete can then be put in and levelled. The levelling is a two person job. A board is tapped along and across the concrete in a series of short and quick movements. It is surprising how one becomes adept at this. The effect is to bring the water and fine material to the top as well as levelling things up and when finished the concrete should be both level and have a nice smooth finish on it. If getting the finish right worries you then this final mix can be from sharp sand and cement in the same quantities. It possibly will lack just a tiny bit of strength but does help the novice get a better finish.

The base will possibly also become the floor of your workshop. If made as suggested it will remain dry and should be quite level. It will, though, be quite dusty. Concrete always leaves a dusty finish when swept. After the building is erected on it this can be cured in several ways. A proprietary sealer can be used, or a special paint. Both will stop the dust and will allow the floor to be cleaned. The paint is possibly the best, although it works out dearer and is more difficult to apply. Sealer only need be tipped on and brushed over with a soft broom and allowed to dry. The paint obviously needs to be applied with a roller or brush.

After a sealer has been applied the floor can be covered with vinyl tiles or sheet if one wishes. This gives a good finish and makes for easy cleaning. It also makes the floor much warmer to stand on, as well as preventing damage to some extent if things are dropped. The tiles will absorb just that little bit of impact and I have often been thankful for having tiled my workshop floor. It is something which I have done on three occasions now and I think it a good investment. Another way of tiling the floor which I have done successfully is to lay down hardboard and then lay the tiles on this. There is no need to seal the floor. When I have done it I have always first laid on another damp-proof membrane, and then stuck hardboard down with the tiles on top. It certainly makes a warm floor and does even more to prevent damage when things are dropped on it.

So much for a new floor, but just suppose an old building is being used with a concrete floor already there. It is unlikely that there will be a damp-proof membrane and it is highly possible that it will not be level. Floors that are not level can be fairly easily levelled up with one of the proprietary products that are now available. These are usually based on latex and are remarkably good at finding their own level. They are quite easy to use and well worth considering, although they are a little expensive.

Putting in a damp-proof membrane is almost impossible unless one builds the floor up by several inches. The idea of putting down hardboard on a damp proof membrane will work but fungus will tend to collect on the underside of the plastic sheet. A good fungicide should therefore first of all be brushed over the floor and allowed to soak in thoroughly. If some fungicide powder can also be sprinkled down all well and good. The idea works and I have done it and when the boarding was lifted several years later no harm had come of it although the plastic sheeting had a lot of damp on the underside.

If the floor can be built up, so well and good, and we can at this stage not only make it damp-proof but warm as well. A framework of 50mm × 50mm wood with plenty of cross pieces is made up and laid on the concrete floor with damp coursing under the wood. Damp coursing is a black bituminous material bought in strips. The area between the wooden framework can be filled with insulating granules and then a floor laid over the top, flooring quality chipboard being a good medium for the actual flooring. The end result is very warm and cosy. Personally I do not think it a good idea to put fibreglass or similar material in the space because of the damp. However, if that material is preferred then use the idea of the fungicide and the damp-proof membrane over the whole floor and everything should work out all right.

Existing wooden floors or those bought with wooden sectionalised buildings may need strengthening to take the weight of machinery. This can usually be done by putting in extra battens and then an extra overlay of chipboard. In the case of the floorboards for sectionalised buildings, a layer of insulation material underneath will work wonders as far as comfort is concerned.

Roofing

The roof of our workshop will be of the utmost importance. Apart from the obvious point of keeping the weather out we need to think of keeping warmth in, as well as maintenance. If an existing building is being used then we have little choice in the roof shape, although that probably will not really matter. With a new building, whether purchased or home built, we frequently will be able to choose the shape of roof we require. Basically the roof will either be a pointed or apex type or the flat or pent type; such a roof is not really flat as some slope must be allowed for water to get away. But we will deal with the construction and the advantages and disadvantages of the two types as we go along.

Let us start with the use of an existing building, other than part

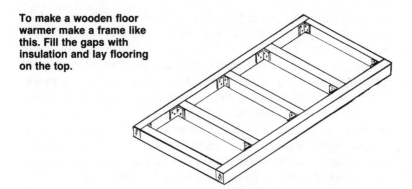

To make a wooden floor warmer make a frame like this. Fill the gaps with insulation and lay flooring on the top.

of the house but including the garage. The roof should be looked at before getting machinery installed. Make sure that it is sound. If you are lucky enough to have a barn with a tiled roof then check that all the tiles are there and if any are missing replace them. Check also the supporting timbers to make sure that none have rotted. It is easier to change them at this stage than it will be after the workshop is set out.

It is far more likely that most people will have a roof of felt. These have a very limited life and particularly in the case of the pent roof the felt starts to blister and become porous, which means that it either leaks or will do so shortly. There are two choices – either strip the roofing felt off and start again, in which case the advice for roof building applies, or make repairs. Fortunately with modern materials that are available this can now be done fairly easily.

Assuming that repair has been decided on then first of all cut the felt where it is blistered, two ways to form a cross, so that the four corners can be lifted up. Make sure that the weather is fine before you start. Allow the underneath of the felt to dry if it happens to be wet; this drying can be accentuated with a portable hair dryer. The next step is to coat the underneath of the cut felt with one of the proprietary roof sealing compounds that are available and then to press the felt back in position. It should be allowed to dry thoroughly. When all the bubbles have been treated the roof can either have another layer of felt put on it or it can be completely painted over with a sealing compound specially sold for the purpose. There is a whole range of these available on the market from builders' merchants. Another alternative is to cover the roof with bitumastic compound and then to scatter special reflective stones on it. These have the effect of throwing the heat of the sun back and so preventing further blistering.

If a prefabricated shed is bought then usually the roof is supplied already felted and it is just a case of following the manufacturer's instructions. If a prefabricated garage type building, the same might apply, or the roof might be some form of corrugated sheeting. Again it should be fixed according to the manufacturer's instructions. We do really need to do some other work though. A big heat loss will occur through the roof and so before fitting it some form of insulation should be incorporated. In the case of the wooden shed glass fibre or rockwool should be put between the joists and held in position with string wrapped round nails. When the roof is finally fixed the joists can have insulation board or some similar material screwed to them on the inside. It may not be possible to carry this out before fixing the roof if the building is on the large side because of the increase in weight. It may also be difficult to locate the roof after the insulation has been fixed to it. In these cases the insulation will have to be fitted when the roof is in position. There is nothing wrong with this method: it is just more difficult trying to push the insulation material in to the spaces from underneath.

Prefabricated concrete buildings such as garages or sheds usually have angle iron trusses. The roof is laid on these and held with bolts, possibly with a hook to go under the edge of the angle iron. Unfortunately this form of construction makes it almost impossible to fit the insulation before fitting the roof in position and it must be left until afterwards, when wood will have to be fixed to the angle iron on which to fix the inner roof or ceiling.

A third material that may be come across as a roofing medium is corrugated pvc sheeting. I am sure this is quite familiar to most readers. This material is either held to wooden joists with special nails or to angle irons with hook bolts. It is quite a good roofing material and it allows light in. It suffers very badly from letting the heat out. Filling in underneath with glass fibre wool and insulation board prevents heat loss but of course stops the light getting in. One solution is to put a second layer of the same material over the top of the original one with a gap of about an inch in between so that in effect we have double glazing. This allows the light in. It also stops the other problem with this type of roof, which is condensation. If one layer alone is left on a workshop, after the workshop has been used the inside of the roof will be running with condensation. It is not therefore a suitable medium unless preca-utions are taken against this, but if properly dealt with it has many advantages, particularly in a workshop that gets used more during the day than at night.

Because of its nature corrugated pvc sheeting leaves gaps along the joints where it is fixed to the walls and these obviously will allow cold air in. They can be filled with special foam rubber that is sold for the purpose or with an expanding filler such as Solvite which is now available. The latter is a much more permanent solution to the problem.

If we are constructing our own building then we will have to make the roof for ourselves. We can still have the choice of a pitch or pent roof, and rafters will need to be laid on accordingly. In the case of a pent roof, in order to fix the rafters to the walls wood can be secured to the tops of the walls and the rafters fitted to this. If the building is made of wood then of course this is already there as part of the structure. Another way of holding them in if the building is of brick is to leave gaps in the brickwork for them to drop into and then fill in with mortar to hold them down.

For a pitched roof much the same applies. It is possible to purchase brackets that will hold the rafters to brickwork as well as to wood. These are available from any good builders' merchants. Notice that I specify builders' merchants as against DIY shops, which do not always deal with materials such as we are talking about.

Before putting the outer roofing materials in place line the inside of the rafters and put insulating materials in place. If electrical wiring is going in the roof it should be put in at this stage, and indeed should always be put in at the time of insulation anyway. The outer part of the roof can then be put on.

We want boarding on the rafters. This can be either a heavy quality chipboard or tongued and grooved timber. It can be secured with nails to the rafters but screwing is much stronger. Next cover the whole roof with a single sheet of polythene sheeting of as heavy a quality as possible; should the roof be too large for this (and it would have to be pretty large as the sheeting is sold in twelve feet widths to any length) then an overlap of at least twelve inches should be allowed and this should be sealed with a transparent tape that is available for the purpose. Do not nail the sheeting to the roof, just lay it on and trim it to size. Should the weather be windy stick the corners down with an impact adhesive.

INSULATING MATERIAL
BETWEEN RAFTERS

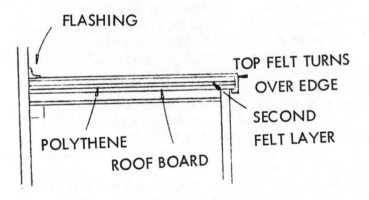

FLASHING

TOP FELT TURNS
OVER EDGE

SECOND
FELT LAYER

POLYTHENE

ROOF BOARD

This can now be covered with two layers of heavy duty roofing felt. These are laid in opposite directions. The overlap amount should be indicated on the wrappers and the overlap should be stuck down with a bitumastic compound. The felt can then be pulled underneath the edge of the roof and nailed in position with the special large headed nails sold for this purpose. The polythene sheeting will ensure that should the felt wear then the roof will not leak.

In the case of a brick building or one made of building blocks, a barge board should be screwed in position along the top of the wall butting up against the inside of the roof. Later this can be sealed with a sealing compound to prevent damp or draughts from entering. Guttering should be fixed in position on this or, in the case of a wooden shed, on the wooden walls. Guttering is advisable to prevent the walls of the building getting damp. Drain pipes from it should be run into a soakaway. This is a hole filled with brick rubble and then covered over again. The brick rubble ensures that water soaks down in to the ground instead of remaining on the surface. Guttering can be comparatively light-weight plastic type.

Many ready-made buildings do not have guttering and while it is desirable it is not an absolute necessity. If the building is to be left without it the edge of the roof should overlap the walls by at least six inches to allow water to fall clear of the walls as far as possible.

If the workshop is to be of the lean-to type attached to the house or some other building, the join between the roof and the wall of the existing building will have to be sealed. Rain is remarkable in the way it will find its way in through any little gap that is left. We do this with what is known as flashing. Traditionally thin sheet zinc was used for the purpose but nowadays mastic sheeting is quite often employed. Do not skimp on the width of the flashing. It is fixed to the house wall and bent round and over the roof of the workshop. The advantage of mastic sheeting is that it can be stuck in position. There is still some danger of leaks, though, and so care must be taken to ensure that it is properly sealed, particularly along the house wall. If zinc sheeting is used, a part-layer of the mortar in the house brickwork can be removed and the sheeting tucked into the gap. New mortar can then be fed in to seal the zinc sheeting off. Alternatively it can be sealed either with or without the mortar removal with a special adhesive strip that can be bought.

That shows how to set about making the roof waterproof, but what is the advantage or disadvantage of the two types? The pent roof means less overhead space and so less heating will be needed. It also has advantages if you want to put in strip lighting as it can be screwed direct to the rafters. It is possibly also easier to construct if you are making your own. It does tend to wear quicker than the apex type as the water lies on it longer and this causes deterioration of the felt. Sunshine also causes some deterioration and with a pent roof it can get at the whole roof all day where as with the apex roof it may only be on it half the day.

The apex roof definitely causes heating costs to rise. How much will depend largely on how well insulated it is. One advantage it has is that the apex can be used for storage purposes. Shelving can be put in the roofing area for items that are not used too frequently. It makes a useful metal storage area as well and several people I know keep their metal there. So it is really again a case of personal choice and the reader must make the decision for him or her self. Possibly the only advice can be that the apex roof might be more suitable for the woodworker or model engineer who is more likely to use the storage space, the pent roof will suit the clockmaker and boat modeller with less need for storage.

5 LAYOUT

When deciding to obtain or build the new workshop, or before moving in to an existing building if possible, things should be carefully planned out as regards the layout. What goes where and why is most important. For example, grinding machines should be kept well clear of other machinery and if at all possible shielded from them in some way or another. Asking oneself which will be the most used area is a useful idea. There is little point in putting a machine in front of a window giving valuable light if it will only be used once a year.

Tool racks should have the tools situated in such a way that they relate to the immediately adjacent area. No point in putting milling cutters etc. by the hand bench where they will rarely be used – get them by the correct machine. If a machine is to go in a certain place, before putting it there ask yourself whether or not it will be practical. Even after all this planning there is still a chance that there will have to be some movement to get everything right. Moving heavy machinery about is no joke, though, and so every effort should be made to get that sorted out from the word go.

One way of getting things right is to make up a planning chart. Use squared paper of the type used for making graphs, or rule a piece up into convenient sized squares, each square to represent a measurement which will be related to the workshop. Mark in the position of doors and windows, then get a couple of postcards or an empty cereal packet and cut out shapes to represent the various machines, benches, heaters etc. to exactly the same scale. Several pleasant hours can be spent laying these on the plan and deciding what fits where. Mark the plan with the position of electric sockets and lighting, unless these will be changed, and in this way it is possible to get a good idea of the best place to put things.

A similar idea can be carried out by making a plan of each wall showing windows etc. and making cut-outs of shelving loaded with whatever has to be stored on them, as well as any cupboards that will hang on the wall. It is surprising how this planning can help when it comes to the time to move in. It may be that like me you will want to carry out brazing operations or something else in another place. For example I use the garage. Gas cylinders are very heavy and there is no point storing them a long way from where they are to be used. If they cannot be stored where needed get them as close as possible.

At this stage the more thought that is given to the layout the better. We all want to rush in and get started but it is asking for trouble. I have already pointed out that some things are bound not to be right even when thought is given to their location, and in fact I found that a cabinet I built for my grinding machines needed moving not long after I had settled in to the new workshop. The least movement the better and so plan, plan and plan again.

Storage

Where to put things so that they are readily accessible is an eternal problem in the small workshop. There never seems to be quite enough room and as the years go on more and more things are acquired that we keep in case they are going to come in handy at some time. Of course many of these are not used and after a few years are thrown away, only to be just what was needed a week or two later. Careful attention to storage will certainly help when it comes to the ability to store things that are or might be needed.

For the metal worker a big problem is metal. It is awkward stuff to keep and yet if we do not hold some in stock there is the

Planning a workshop layout

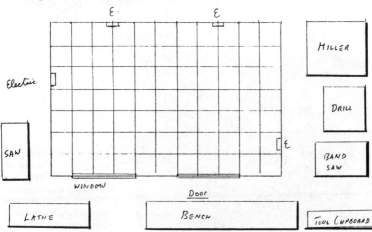

This is part of Ian Cherry's workshop and shows how metal is stored in square plastic drain pipes.

everlasting chore of trying to get what is required when we need it, and if no stockist is nearby there will almost invariably be a waiting period while the metal comes through the post. How to store it will depend largely on what lengths are kept. Short lengths can be kept under benches and I would suggest that it is done in such a way that the metal is made easily accessible. Just putting all of it in one rack leads to absolute frustration. It is difficult to see just what is in stock at any one time and in my experience hunting through metal racks for a particular size just results in a heap of metal crashing on to the floor.

A useful metal rack can be made from square plastic rain water piping. This is fairly cheap and can be purchased easily at either a

Stack of drawers for small items, stubs of metal etc. in Ted Jolliffe's workshop. Such drawers may be found in a second-hand dealer's shop

DIY store or a builders' merchants. it can be cut into suitable lengths and these held together to form a rectangle, rather as one sees a rack for wine bottles. The metal ends are then facing the front of the bench and what is in stock is easily seen. Plastic guttering screwed to the walls or underneath the benches is also useful material for the storage of metal. Because of its shape; however, it is not quite so easy to use as is the square drain piping.

For longer lengths a rack can be made along a wall. Keep it somewhere where the contents can be seen, although if the stock held in it will not be used too often it can be put fairly high or very low down where it will allow the wall to be used for purposes other than just to hold a metal rack. I know of several model engineers who keep their metal in racks suspended from the ceiling, and providing it has adequate strength then there is no reason why not. Guttering and drain piping can be screwed to the ceiling with suitable brackets.

Very small pieces of metal will need to be stored differently and I would suggest that narrow drawers are possibly the best answer to these. They can be kept in small boxes on shelving. Unfortunately small ends of metal tend to build up if we are not careful and so it is essential that they are kept in a place where they can be easily seen so that the temptation to cut a piece off a longer length because it is easier to do so is avoided. The larger sized pieces in short lengths can be kept on shelves under benches. There are not usually too many of these and they can all be stacked together ready for use, possibly somewhere near to a machine where they may be needed.

The woodworker will need similar storage facilities for the storage of timber. This is bulkier than metal although nowhere

Plastic drawer units enable GLR Distributors to find immediately any of the hundreds of small items they stock. A workshop can benefit in exactly the same way!

near as heavy. Storage racks attached to ceilings are possibly as good an answer as any, with, in this case, short lengths stored on shelves in such a way that they are easily visible.

Storage of wood or metal standing upright against a wall is another way of dealing with longer lengths. There is nothing wrong with the method if the material is to be used in the near future. Both wood and metal will warp if stood in this way for any length of time. The heavier the section of course the longer it will stand this sort of treatment.

Tools should be kept in racks if at all possible. Some tools which will not frequently be in use can be kept in drawers but it is better to keep them where they can be seen if possible. If the racks can be incorporated in a narrow cupboard then all well and good, this will also help to keep the tools in good condition. Never make tool cupboards deep as it becomes difficult to get at and to replace tools kept at the back and all to easy to leave them out of the cupboard in case they are going to be used in the near future. There is also a tendency with deep cupboards to just put things in the front and in this way when a tool is required from the back a lot of stuff has to be removed to get at it.

If benches have been fitted with doors then the inside of such

Bernie Buckland makes extensive use of pegboard for tool storage. Hooks can readily be bought or made.

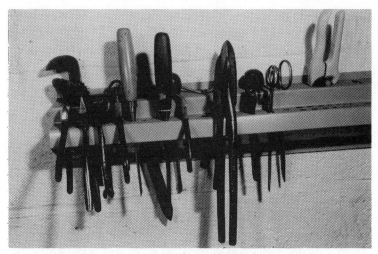

An inexpensive form of commercial tool rack keeps the tools in one place, if slightly jumbled. Usefulness depends on number of tools.

doors makes useful space for tool racks. Obviously the tools so stored should not be so heavy as to cause the door hinges to sag but even so it is surprising just how much can be kept in this way. Files are one obvious commodity to store in racks on the inside of doors. Whatever happens files should never be stored in drawers where they will tend to rub against each other and so lose their sharpness.

Another type of commercial rack with clip-on front plates to hold various tools. Centre plate is for screwdrivers, chisels etc.

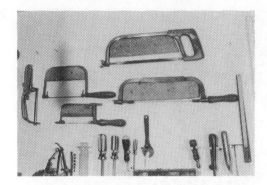

Cut out shapes not only support tools securely but show at a glance if one is missing.

For the storage of very small items some of the excellent little plastic box sets now available are ideal. The contents can clearly be labelled and with the small drawers there is little wasted space. Tobacco tins are very good for keeping screws etc in and they too can be clearly labelled. The square type will fit together neatly and when put on a very narrow shelf make a very useful and easily accessible means of storage.

It can be worth looking round for old disused furniture to use for storage purposes. Old kitchen wall units can be used to advantage though some are a bit deep for the workshop. Even so the use of such a thing saves a lot of work and if need be the width could quite easily be cut down. Chests of drawers can be pressed into service. The drawers are often rather on the large side but are ideal for holding drawings and can be partitioned off to take tools. It is also possible to convert the deeper drawers in to two or more layers by putting in some plywood. This avoids tools being laid on top of each other which makes it difficult to get at the one required.

The making of simple racks for tools is quite easy and a purpose-built rack is possibly better than anything that is adapted. I also make cut-outs of various tools which I screw to walls as a

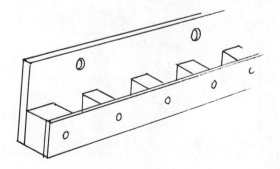

Simple tool rack construction.

Bob Moore has a drilled plank over the lathe with hooks for tools, holes for chuck keys etc.

means of holding them and find that in so doing there is never any question of tools being misplaced.

Drills, taps reamers etc. should always be stored in some form of a rack and never in drawers or tins. Keeping them all together in this way causes them to rub against each other and lose their sharpness. If for any reason such tools are kept in tins or drawers then they should first be wrapped in paper to prevent damage. I keep any spare items in this way but those to be used are all kept in racks. Some of these racks consist of no more than a block of wood with appropriate sized holes drilled in it. This is quite effective and can be added to as one wishes.

In this book there are a number of photographs of people's

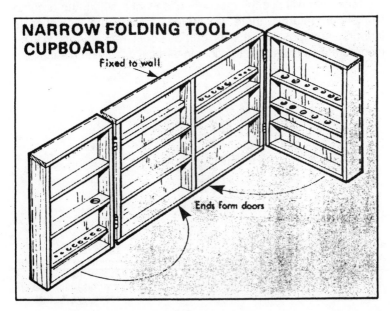

NARROW FOLDING TOOL CUPBOARD

Fixed to wall

Ends form doors

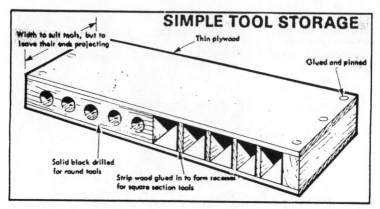

SIMPLE TOOL STORAGE

Width to suit tools, but to leave their ends projecting

Thin plywood

Glued and pinned

Solid block drilled for round tools

Strip wood glued in to form recesses for square section tools

workshops. All these workshops are those of very experienced modellers. The reader can do no better than study these and see how these people have solved their problems of storage. Remember when this part of the job is planned that there will be a need to find things easily and quickly. Leaving tools or anything else likely to be required piled up in boxes or drawers is not the answer. Neatness is the best way to get things sorted out so that the maximum benefit can be obtained from our workshops.

The Interior
No matter what type of building is being used the interior will be the thing that will occupy most attention when setting up a home workshop. Naturally there will be less to do if the workshop is indoors, and possibly if it is purpose-built refinements will be incorporated into its construction. In particular a building such as a

Drills, taps etc. should never be kept in tins. Keep them in a wood block like these needle files.

The interior of a workshop should be kept neat and tidy if it is to be efficient. This picture shows the inside of a workshop belonging to Henry Hartley. Everything is neatly laid out and easy to get at. Note the usual theme of small storage units in the form of drawers and how files are kept in a rack.

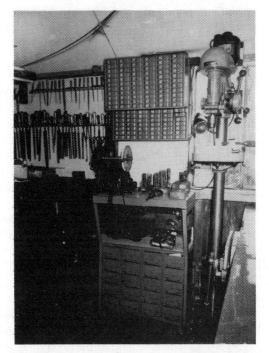

garden shed or an old barn being adapted for the purpose will be in need of having work carried out on the interior. Many people sadly neglect this side of things and put up with working in draughty and possibly damp conditions, not to mention having considerable extra expense if the building is to be heated.

It is most important to reduce heat loss to a minimum. This not only gives economy but also makes the building much more comfortable to use, as well as reducing the rusting problem. Let us then see how we can set about gaining some of this comfort.

Windows and doors should be the first priority. If possible an effort should be made to double glaze the windows. This need not be a terribly expensive item as it is possible to use some form of secondary double glazing. The difference this makes is quite incredible. As this is being written I have not long moved into a new house, the new workshop being the rear of the double garage. The first job was to carry out much of the advice I will be giving, which I knew from experience was needed. Time was short, however, and winter set in with the windows still not dealt with. It proved to be a very hard winter and in spite of an efficient heating system, when working near the windows, even those that did not open, it was considerably colder than was the rest of the workshop. As a temporary measure I pinned some plastic sheeting to the window frames, so that it covered the windows. This simple form of double glazing made a vast difference to the warmth of the workshop.

The method looked untidy and it will be replaced during the better weather. It can be replaced in a variety of ways. It is possible to purchase special plastic or alloy sections designed to be used as double glazing and these are cut to size and fixed round the window frames. Glass is inserted making a neat double glazing unit. If windows open then it is possible to obtain special parts to allow the double glazing units to open as well. The systems are very effective and are not all that expensive to buy. They are also very easy to install.

Another method is to fix glass inside the existing window frames using wooden beading. If possible the glass should in this case be sealed round the edges with a foam rubber strip. The required beading is easy to obtain and it is not difficult to make it into suitable frames to take the glass. It can be just as effective as the purpose-bought double glazing sections.

The use of heavy plastic sheeting is worth considering and there are several types of framework available for this. Some allow the plastic sheeting to be fixed magnetically which makes it easy to remove for cleaning. Others allow for the sheeting to be

An earlier workshop of the author's. Walls and ceiling are panelled and there is insulation 4in. thick behind the panels. Windows are an ideal height. Note doors beneath lathe to keep things clean.

fixed in frames. Yet another system makes use of the thin plastic film used for cooking and known as clingfilm. This is fixed with an attachment and afterwards heated with a hair dryer which makes it go taut. The system is not permanent as the clingfilm needs replacing from time to time. It is very cheap to buy and the framing can be used time and time again.

If using plastic try and get hold of the correct type of sheeting if possible. Normal polythene sheeting goes brittle in sunlight and so will not last too long if used for double glazing purposes. A special polythene sheeting is made for the purpose and if this is obtained it will last for years. It is also possible to buy some types of thin plastic film designed to keep the sun's heat to a minimum if this should be a problem. I have had a workshop in the past where the sun caused quite a few problems, and so whilst it is nice to bask in its heat and to enjoy the light given it is possible to have too much of a good thing.

Draughts are a big problem and make working very difficult at times. Draught-excluding strip that can be stuck round doors and windows is easily available and well worth while fitting. There are a variety of types ranging from a cheap foam strip to a plastic channelling with fine hairs moulded in. This type I find particularly good for keeping the place warm. The bottom of the door or doors should not be forgotten either; again there are plenty of draught-

Neat workshop belonging to Tony Challon, built of breeze blocks. Note window height, which gives clearance above the bench.

Shelves behind author's lathe hold ready-to-use accessories. Upper shelf is drilled for Morse taper tools to prevent rolling about.

proofing strips available to seal this off and it is one of the areas most likely to cause trouble.

Floors and roofs have been dealt with elsewhere but the question of walls has not and we should certainly give these some thought. In our homes walls are always insulated in some way or another. It may just be an air cavity in them or they may be of very thick brick or stone. Some will have insulation in the wall cavities. Our workshops should be treated similarly. Wooden walls are cold. Other types of material used for building suffer similar defects. If at all possible insulating the walls is a wise precaution and again it is quite surprising the difference it makes. Some form of insulation material inserted between an inner and outer wall is best.

Most workshops do not of course have inner and outer walls and we must in this case create our own. If battens are fixed vertically on the walls at intervals of say half a metre or eighteen inches then it is possible to cover this with an insulating material and to fill the cavity with some insulation such as glass fibre.

The battens should be made of comparatively wide timber. This makes it easier to locate when nailing or screwing the inner walling material to it. I also leaves plenty of room for fixing shelf

Rolled newspaper hung between exterior and interior walls is a cheap but effective form of insulation

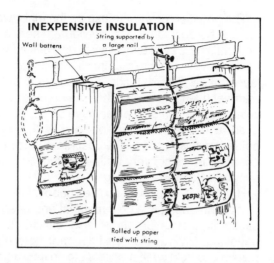

INEXPENSIVE INSULATION

String supported by a large nail

Wall battens

Rolled up paper tied with string

brackets etc. Suppose we use 30mm × 30mm timber for the battens. Then when fixing the inner walls we have to be very careful to get within the limits of the wood with our nails or screws. This is difficult enough but when it comes to fixing shelving brackets the screws of which will have to go right through the inner lining and into the battens, a great deal of skill is neded to get things right. If for our batten we use 30m × 50 or even 75mm timber then the location becomes a great deal easier. I have used old floorboards for the purpose. Purchased second-hand they were both cheap and easy to use and the extra width made a great deal of difference.

I have suggested the use of glass fibre as an insulation material but there are alternatives. One good one is newspapers. They can be rolled up and held with string and make excellent insulation material for walls. Polystyrene foam is another alternative, although I must confess I am not keen on the material personally as I consider it something of a fire risk. This is only a personal opinion and it can and often is used for such purposes.

Before laying the inner wall in place make sure that you have all the electric wires you need in position and that suitable holes are made for them to come through into the workshop. It may also be necessary to put some extra wooden battens in position to support such things as electric sockets, light switches etc. It is most unlikely that the material used for the inner walls will have sufficient strength to support these and so when they are fitted screws should go right through the inner wall and into the wood behind.

The question of what to use as the inner walling is one that will have to be decided by the individual. There are a whole variety of materials now available. Plaster board is a form of boarding made up of plaster of paris in a special form, sandwiched between two layers of cardboard. It comes in a variety of thicknesses. It is the material used internally in houses on most occasions, and if dealt with properly can give a very nice finish. But remember when it is used in houses it is laid on to a wall and not usually just on battening. It is not I feel the best material for workshops as it does not support weight very well. Anything fixed to it would have to be supported on the battening.

Hardboard. This is by far the cheapest material but it has many disadvantages. It is a cold material and even when insulated can cause condensation. It is also difficult to lay flat along the battening. Even so if cost is important it is worth consideration. It is possible to hold shelf brackets etc. to it by using one of the special forms of securing devices now sold for the purpose.

Chipboard is a very strong material and can be used for walling quite easily. It is easy to fix to battening but should be screwed to them rather than nailed. It will support light objects but for shelves etc. that are likely to take any amount of weight then a suitable patent securing device should be used or the screws should be passed right through into the battening.

The use of insulation board has much to recommend it. It is like a thick paper and does not have a great deal of strength. It is easy to fix and as its name suggests it supplies insulation. In fact it is very warm to the touch. Once again it will not support brackets etc. and the patent fasteners that can be used with chipboard and hardboard are not at all successful with it. Screws used for supporting purposes on shelving must therefore be put right through into the battening.

None of these materials is very good when it comes to painting. All absorb the paint very quickly. It follows then that all will need to be covered with several coats of emulsion paint in order to improve their appearance. Another alternative is to treat them with one of the proprietary sealing compounds before applying paint. Walls in workshops must be treated with either a paint or some form of covering so that splashes of oil and other liquids do not get absorbed by the material that has been used.

6   BENCHES AND VICES

Benches

The heart of the workshop is its bench, at which many pleasant hours will be spent. Let us then make sure that this is suitably made and sited. Personally I always like daylight by my bench and so site it as near to a window as possible. That of course must be the choice of the individual.

Wherever the bench is going to be it will need to be rigid and thought should be given to this. It is not impossible to work on a bench that has the shakes but it does make life more difficult and so the order of the day must be to make it as rigid as possible.

For those not wishing to make a bench there is quite a range available on the market. Most are aimed at the woodworker or do-it-yourself enthusiast rather than the model engineer, but there are some which will suit the model engineer. Many of the DIY stores have benches on sale that can be put to use. They are sometimes a little flimsy but can easily be brought up to standard. The thing that will make most benches rigid is securing them to walls and wherever possible this should be done. By so doing it is possible to make the bench of a much lighter construction than if it is to be free-standing.

The woodworker's bench will differ from the metal worker as a rule. More often than not the woodworking bench is made with a well along the middle and a flat plank down the side. It includes such items as bench stops and sometimes a built-in wood vice.

Whatever the bench is to be used for, it must be given as much strength as it can and care must be taken to try and get a really solid top on it. Suitable materials for this are not easily come by and so it might be necessary to use several layers of material. If possible the top should be at least 35mm or 1½ inches thick. A good way of getting this sort of thickness is to use layers of chipboard. If the thickness can be increased beyond those measurements so well and good.

The finish on top of the bench is important too. If chipboard is

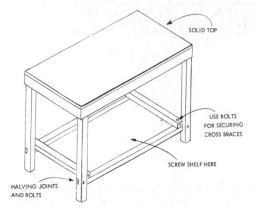

Typical bench construction. The heavier the timbers the better, and clamping or screwing to a wall aids rigidity.

SOLID TOP

USE BOLTS
FOR SECURING
CROSS BRACES

SCREW SHELF HERE

HALVING JOINTS
AND BOLTS

left plain it will soon start to show signs of wear. It will also rapidly absorb anything that may have been spilt on it. It must be either painted or varnished to stop this happening. Another idea is to make the top layer from a piece of the plastic covered chipboard. This is not suitable though if the bench is to be used for heavy work as the plastic will crack and chip. It is ideal for a bench that will be used for marking out or drawing, and it can be used successfully under machinery which is bench mounted.

If possible, and if there is room, a bench should be set aside for marking-out operations and other clean work. If room is not available then a piece of board can be kept specially for the

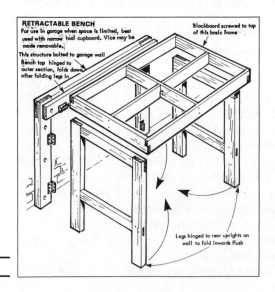

RETRACTABLE BENCH
For use in garage when space is limited, best used with narrow tool cupboard. Vice may be made removable.
This structure bolted to garage wall
Bench top hinged to outer section, folds down after folding legs in

Blockboard screwed to top of this basic frame

Legs hinged to rear uprights on wall to fold inwards flush

Sometimes a folding bench has to be accepted. Sturdiness is then a matter of timber and hinge sizes.

The Sjoberg 1200 bench basically for woodwork but adaptable. Grips work in two places.

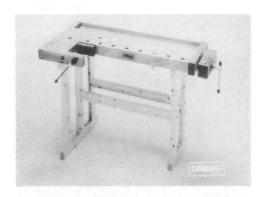

The Sjoberg 1422 bench grips work in three places. Cupboard and drawer unit strengthens an already rigid bench.

The Dunlop Powerbase and the well-known B&D Workmate are portable but rigid benches. Useful for bandsaws and sanding machines, supporting work in progress and many other purposes.

One of a series of bolt-together benches by HTS Structural Products. Iron-framed, they include tool racks on doors and pegboard-type back; a light can be incorporated along the top. May be free-standing or fixed.

purpose. For those indulging in hobbies such as jewellery-making or clockmaking the clean bench or board could be covered with green baize material to good effect. It is now possible to purchase this material with an adhesive backing which makes it easy to use.

The frame of the bench can be made either of heavy wood or of steel, slotted angle being a suitable medium. This bolts together and is easy to use as well as being rigid. If making the frame of wood do not be tempted to nail it together. It should not even be screwed but should be joined with bolts being passed right through the timbers and tightened up. In use the bench has to withstand a great deal of vibration and this will shake loose timber that has been nailed or screwed. It may possibly cause the bolts to come loose as well but these can easily be tightened up.

The bench should be built at a height to suit the individual, taking into account the height that the vice will be above it. It is not a good idea to have deep benches and about eighteen inches is usually as deep as it will need to be, unless it is required to support some particular machine or other that is of a greater width than this. Shelving secured underneath will all help with rigidity, but there is little need to bolt this in position and wood screws will do the job just as well.

Personally I like to put doors on benches which have things stored underneath them. It is not so important if drawers have been fitted but otherwise it offers protection to whatever is stored underneath. Iron and other metal filings seem to get everywhere if care is not taken and a simple door can prevent a great deal of trouble. There is no need for any complicated woodwork to make the doors, an ordinary piece of chipboard with a couple of hinges will do the job, and a bit of paint will stop oil soaking in. If the bench is made of steel then it may be that a wooden strip will need to be bolted on to the uprights in order that the door hinges can be secured to it.

The Vice

If the bench is the heart of the workshop, the vice or vices that we will install will run it very close in importance. Of course no matter how good the vice is unless it is mounted on a sturdy bench then a great deal of its value will be diminished. Those with a temporary space who are having to pick up and put down their work will need to buy a vice with either a suction fitting or a clamp that will hold it to the table or whatever is being used as a bench. This of necessity will mean the use of a vice of somewhat smaller capacity than one might wish for, but it is possible to purchase both suction and clamp type vices in sizes up to three inches. The size by the way refers to the width of the jaws and not the amount by which the vice will open. A three inch vice for example will usually open some four or more inches.

If permanent premises are available then care should be taken with the selection of the vice if possible. My own personal feeling is that the minimum size needed is four inches, and then if there is room in the workshop a smaller one can be installed to take care

An engineer's swivel-based steel vice from Warren Machine Tools. From 3–6in. jaw width. Note small anvil.

This vice holds to a bench via a suction pad and is useful for the workshop that has to be dismantled.

of the more fiddly jobs. It is always possible to make small additional clamps or vices that will go in the big one to look after the smaller jobs.

Most of us are familiar with the engineer's vice. This differs from that of the woodworker in that it is mounted on the top of the bench whereas the woodworker's vice goes at the side or face of the bench. It is no good buying a good solid vice and fitting it to a good solid bench unless it is fitted in a good solid way. It must therefore be bolted to the bench using as large a diameter bolts as possible. Screwing it down is not good practice, as with use the screws will work loose. So will the bolts, but they can easily be tightened up when this happens.

Most engineers' vices follow more or less the same pattern. There are some differences. For example it is possible to purchase a vice that can be swivelled round on a base. This is quite a useful feature and worth considering. Normally hammering of work should not be carried out on the vice as it is not constructed for this purpose, and there is a distinct possibility of cracking the casting. There are some available, though, with a small anvil

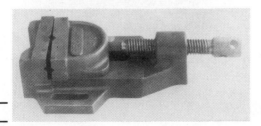

A small drilling vice from Record. The movable jaw swivels and vee cuts grip round material. Size is opening, not jaw width.

incorporated in front of the jaws and these are designed to allow for a limited amount of hammering to be done. Again it is a feature worth considering.

Most vices when bought new have serrated jaws to enable a good grip to be obtained on the work. The jaws are also hardened and so when work is held in the vice it will get marked quite badly. To avoid this separate soft jaws of plastic or similar material can be purchased. These certainly stop the marking of work but it is also difficult to locate work accurately in the vice when they are used. If the vice is purchased new it is a good idea to remove the jaws, which are usually only held on with screws, and to make smooth jaws from mild steel. These will grip some work without causing any marking and enable the work to be set accurately in the vice as well.

It is also a good idea to make jaws from brass and lead as well and then we have a range of jaws which will enable almost anything to be gripped without marking it. Making the jaws is only a matter of drilling a couple of holes and so should present no problems to the average person.

For drilling and similar operations vices are available with flat bases. These allow the work to be put in the vice which can then be stood on the drilling table for whatever operation is to be carried out on it.

Similar vices are also available for milling operations. These are considerably stronger and heavier to allow for the extra pressure that will be put on them when milling operations are to be carried out. It is possible to use a drilling vice on lighter operations in the

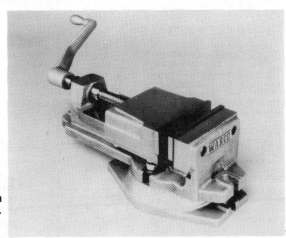

A swivel-based milling vice which can be had in 4in. and 6in. opening from Warren.

milling machine, but there is a possibility of loss of accuracy because of the vice not having the required rigidity.

Some drilling vices are available that allow work to be tilted at an angle should this be required. There are also some referred to as 'cross vices'. These are fixed to a compound slide and enable work to be held in the vice while it is moved around on the drilling machine. There is a lot to be said for the idea, particularly if drilling rows of holes which need to be perfectly lined up. It may also be possible to use such a device for very light milling operations.

When buying a vice of whatever type, try and get the best quality that can be afforded. Some cheaper ones become very sloppy after a while, and when a vice is purchased it should be bought for life. There is not a great deal can be done to test the vice being purchased other than to tighten it up very hard to see if the lead screw will slip under pressure. At the same time the alignment of the jaws can be checked. One obvious way of ensuring quality is to buy a well-known and well-tried make. There are some vices around, though, that are very good value and extremely strong and accurate while not being of what one might call a standard make. Check that the casting is of good thick material and that it is not flimsy. A good guide is often that the heavier the vice for a given size the better the strength of it.

Brazing and Welding Area

The model engineer will certainly wish to carry out soldering, brazing and possibly welding operations in his or her workshop. It is more than probable that those using the workshop for other hobbies will wish to do likewise. It is most desirable that a special area be set aside for such operations. There are various reasons for this. Firstly there is the possibility of fumes, and these fumes

This vice with a compound slide is called a cross-vice. Used for accurate rows of holes or several related holes, on a drilling machine.

Crowhurst Engineering supply brazing hearths made of angle iron and refractory bricks.

can not only be unpleasant to the operator but can also create havoc with tools by causing rust and other oxides to form on metal. Then of course there must with brazing and welding operations be a considerable increase in fire risk. By setting the area aside it is possible to take better fire precautions for that particular place in the workshop.

If possible the area set aside should be as near a door or window as convenient to allow fumes to disperse. A proper bench should be organised. This need not be elaborate but should consist of a steel frame with a heat resistant sheet at the bottom and possibly round the edges, with some refractory fire bricks. By using refractory bricks there is less need to use direct heat on the work, resulting in a cash saving, as well as making it more comfortable for working. Also because they throw the heat back

For small soldering and brazing work a self-contained hand-held torch such as this is adequate.

69

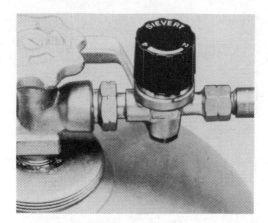

For large work a propane cylinder with a good regulator is desirable.

the fire risk is reduced, as there is less of the heat making contact with walls etc.

If some sort of hood can be organised to extract or at least disperse any fumes that might be generated so well and good. A vacuum cleaner working during operations will clear the air surprisingly well. If this is not possible then a small hood can be made from sheet metal with a compartment for some charcoal grains, the type sold for cooker hoods being ideal. These help no end in disposing of smoke etc. I suppose really there is no reason why a cooker hood should not be purchased and used. These contain fans and although I have never used one personally they would seem to be the ideal thing.

As far as equipment is concerned, for soft soldering, soldering irons of suitable sizes and a small blowlamp will be sufficient. For small brazing operations one of the hand blowlamps operated on butane gas will work quite well. For larger operations, a separate cylinder will be required with a blowlamp and burners that can be changed as required. There is no need to dash out and buy a full set as possibly two or three different sized burners will be suitable for most people.

Oxy-propane or oxy-acetylene torches with the appropriate gas bottles are useful but not essential. There is now quite a range of these, including many more in smaller sizes than was the case previously. It is desirable that such equipment is fitted with

Air and propane regulators allow fine adjustment on this Sievert 3525 burner.

An oxy-propane set such as this will give fierce localised heat and is suitable for many jobs in the field of model engineering and similar pursuits.

pressure gauges as the operation of them depends on using them at the correct pressure. On any gas equipment a feature that should always be fitted is a blow-back valve to prevent lighted gas blowing back down the pipe and causing an explosion in the cylinder. These valves should be fitted whether the equipment is just plain gas or combined with oxygen.

There is an increase in the use of electric welders and there are plenty available for the home market. Some are oil-cooled and others are just air-cooled models. When buying an arc welder the largest capacity possible should be purchased. For welding metal of ⅛ in. or 3mm thick then a welder of a capability of at least 120 amps is really needed and it follows that to weld thicker material a heavier machine is required. More recent additions to the range of welders are the MIG type. These include a canister of inert gas and the welding operation takes place through the gas jet. The result is the ability to weld materials that were previously difficult to cope with, and an improvement on welds on normal materials.

A carbon arc torch is a gadget which fits to an arc welder and by creating an arc between two carbon rods produces a flame that can be used for brazing etc. These are very good for some purposes but are not really suitable for boiler making or similar operations. The system is for many applications a cheap alternative to an oxygen-gas unit.

7 POWER, LIGHTING AND HEATING

Electricity

There can be few workshops these days where there is no electricity supply to run machinery. It is well within living memory that many model engineers worked with treadle-operated lathes and the lucky ones with a hand-operated drilling machine. It was not only model engineers who were somewhat limited in this way. The treadle lathe was used by artificers on ships until well into this century and the hand operated drilling machine was still in use in the early 1960s for people operating on site. The Electricity Companies and the Railways used them intensively.

The next step forward for the hobbyist and model engineer came with the introduction of electricity. In its early days the supply of power was nowhere near as sophisticated as it is now and if a room in a house had one power point then it was well supplied. Usually houses had two circuits, five and fifteen amps. The fifteen was used for power and the five mainly for lighting. There were five amp power points installed in some cases and these took a smaller sized plug, presumably to prevent the overloading of the supply with a heavy cable. All plugs had round prongs and they were not fused in any way.

The model engineer who was running his lathe and other machinery was therefore somewhat limited in the power supply available and it became the custom to fit workshops with line shafts. These were common practice in factories and consisted of shafts running near the ceiling and supplied with power in order that they could rotate. On the shafts were a series of pulleys from which flat belts were run to similar pulleys on each piece of powered equipment to make it work. If one reads back through very old copies of *Model Engineer* and similar magazines there is a wealth of interesting articles on various equipment designed for running this way. Most milling was carried out with a milling spindle operated from an overhead shaft and the lathe saddle was used to mount the work. Very few modellers now use the system, it being far more convenient to have several power points fitted and for each machine to operate with its own motor.

All this may sound like interesting history but the reader must be wondering what it has to do with setting up a modern home workshop. The reason the information has been included is because while we no longer use shafts or have five and fifteen amp sockets the principle remains the same. Lighting circuits should be entirely separate from power. With a line shaft it was usual to operate only one machine at a time and this is good practice even in these days of ample electricity supply.

How our electricity supply is laid into the workshop will depend largely on where the workshop is situated. The power and lighting supplies must be picked up from an existing main. My own personal view is that a power circuit should be tapped and a heavy cable taken to a consumer unit. A consumer unit is the name given to the ordinary switch or fuse box. It consists of a box with a heavy switch and a series of fuses. In some cases these days such a box will include a trip switch which is re-set by pressing a button. This is a far safer arrangement altogether and should be aimed for.

From the consumer unit we should take our various circuits. Each circuit should be fitted with the appropriately rated fuse in the consumer unit, five amps maximum for the lighting circuit and fifteen for the power. The circuits should be made to form a ring. This means that if, say, we start with the lighting circuit, the line cable will be taken to each lighting point in turn and returned to the point at the consumer unit from where it was taken. So we have what amount to two wires leaving that particular terminal. The same applies to the neutral and the earth. The power is dealt with in a similar way. Spurs can be taken off the ring circuits but they should be kept to the minimum.

Wiring should if possible be carried in some form of conduit or trunking. This is usually made in plastic these days and for indoor work plastic conduit is quite suitable. Trunking is like a flat form of conduit the lid of which clips in position after the wires have been

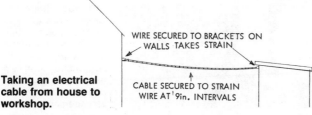

WIRE SECURED TO BRACKETS ON WALLS TAKES STRAIN

CABLE SECURED TO STRAIN WIRE AT 9in. INTERVALS

Taking an electrical cable from house to workshop.

73

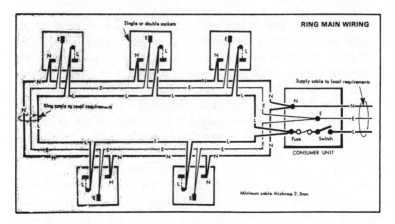

Single or double sockets

Supply cable to local requirements

Ring cable to local requirements

Fuse   Switch

CONSUMER UNIT

Minimum cable thickness 2.5mm

installed. If this cannot be arranged then wires should be securely fixed with proper cable clips at intervals of no more than nine inches. The cable used must be of the correct thickness for the supply being taken: I would suggest at least 1.5mm for lighting and 2.5mm for the power. It is essential to use the wires with their appropriate colours in the correct order – they must not under any circumstances be connected to the wrong terminals.

Where possible double or even treble power sockets should be fitted, and if possible these should be capable of being switched on and off from the sockets rather than being permanently live and relying on the plug being pushed in to make the circuit. In my opinion it is not possible to have too many power points in a workshop. Trailing wires must where possible be avoided and this can only be done by having sufficient points where they are required. Sockets are best situated at or above waist height rather than at floor level. Not only does this make them easier to use but

One would hope never to see a practice such as this. A two way extension is used in conjunction with two two way plugs. An extremely dangerous arrangement.

it also means that wires are not live at ground level. If live wires are left low down there is a very distinct danger of sharp or hot objects falling on them and cutting or burning through with disastrous results.

Having said this we all from time to time will need to use extension leads where somehow or another we do not have a supply available quite where it is needed. Care should be taken that such leads are of adequate thickness and that good quality plugs and sockets are attached. After some use the wires on extension leads have a habit of coming loose and so they should be checked at regular intervals. This applies to the leads connected to all plugs, which will loosen with wear. Extension sockets are available as two, three and four way units and these certainly have some advantages. They should never be wired permanently to the mains supply as they are not designed for this purpose. When extension leads are used the wire if possible should be kept away from gangways etc. where it is likely that it could be tripped over. If the lead is a long one then it should be fully uncoiled while in use. A coiled wire creates extra heat and increases the fire danger.

If a multiple extension lead is used then the total amount of equipment connected to it must not exceed the rating of the original circuit. In other words it is no good connecting a three socket extension on a thirteen amp socket and then putting three heavy duty appliances on the three sockets of the extension. The power taken off must only be the same as would be taken from the normal socket. This also applies to permanently wired multiple sockets.

It is possible to convert a single socket to a double or treble by using a conversion unit like this. The box seen at the top is designed to screw over the existing socket and the treble socket is wired in using the existing wire. Although there is no independent switching the unit is fused.

The use of two way plugs is definitely not to be encouraged. Because of the extra weight applied when additional plugs are fitted there is a tendency for these to become sloppy. A short lead with a double socket is far better. All plugs should be fitted with the correct fuses. These must reflect the current absorbed by the appliance. Fuses are there for protection. If the current absorbed becomes too much for the wiring or the appliance the fuse must blow. If not there is a distinct danger of the wiring overheating and catching fire. For example if a table lamp is fitted to a socket via a plug then there should definitely be a fuse rating of no higher than two amps. If a thirteen amp fuse is fitted the lamp can be overloaded in certain circumstances.

Lighting in the workshop is worth thinking about. Fluorescent lights have both advantages and disadvantages. They give a good overall illumination but the light is continually pulsating. This can strain the eyes but, worse still, with machinery working at certain speeds the effect could be stroboscopic and the rotating machinery appear to be stationary. While such lighting is very useful it should be supplemented near machinery with ordinary tungsten type lighting. This is possibly best obtained from individual lamps of the types known as angle-poise. Such lamps are relatively cheap to buy and they can be swivelled as well as lifted and lowered to direct lighting exactly where it is required. Another alternative is a portable type spotlight. These can be obtained so that they clip on to shelves etc. and the light directed to exactly where it is needed. In industry there is an insistence on low voltage lighting for reasons of safety. Such a feature is desirable in a home workshop but is not often likely to be convenient to arrange.

So much for the actual workshop and how to deal with the electric supply, but what if our workshop is down the garden? The actual fitting out should be dealt with in the way already described. The supply can be carried down the garden in a variety of ways. If the distance to be travelled is not more than, say, six metres then the supply could be taken overhead. There is no need for special cable, the modern type being quite suitable for the purpose. The wire should not just be allowed to drape over the vacant space, however, but should be supported by galvanised wire held firmly to the house and the workshop, electrical cable being bound to this every foot or so of the run.

If the workshop is more than about six metres away then the cable should be buried. It should be placed a minimum of eighteen inches or half a metre in the ground and the trench in which it is

A portable clip-on spotlight like this can be a useful addition to the workshop equipment. The large clip enables it to be held to shelving, brackets, or similar places and the light can be directed exactly where it is required.

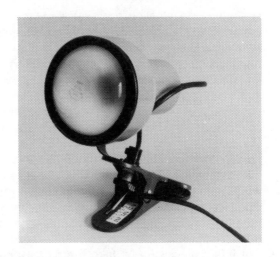

laid filled with gravel to prevent the cable from lying in water. If it is possible to put the cable in a metal conduit then this is better still, since it will prevent any accidental damage at a later date. If a wall is available an alternative is for the cable to be fitted along this with suitable clips at nine inch intervals. It is not desirable to fit a cable along a wooden fence, there always being the danger of this blowing down. If it is to be fixed along one it should be put into metal conduit which is fixed firmly to the fence.

An alternative is to wire the workshop and to fit the consumer unit to a heavy wire with a plug. A heavy duty extension lead can then be made up and run to the workshop as and when required. This is not a terribly satisfactory arrangement but many people do it. Heavy wire should be used for the extension cable and it should be of the exact length required to avoid unnecessary cable lying about.

Some machinery will need three phase electricity and this can be arranged. It is dealt with in the chapter on electric motors.

Finally let me say that all wiring should if possible be carried out before installing insulation etc. in the workshop so that where possible wires can run through the double skinning of the walls rather than on the outside. If you are in any doubt whatever consult a qualified electrician. Electricity can kill.

Heating
If the workshop is to be used during cold weather then the question of heating it must be considered. My research seems to indicate that workshops are used more in winter than in summer

so the heating question is obviously of the greatest importance. If the workshop is indoors and the house is centrally heated then the problem is taken care of. My own present workshop, at the rear of a garage which is attached to the house, has a radiator which was installed by the previous owner and very useful it is, too. I think that it was possibly the clinching factor in the house purchase! It is possible to take a radiator into a workshop that is not directly connected to the house and in fact a friend of mine did just that. The lengths of piping required were not all that great and he was able to bury them under the ground after making sure they were suitably lagged. The lagging was about four times as thick as would normally be expected in order to prevent heat loss and the pipes were laid in a trench of pebbles so that water would not stay round them. The lagging was also needed of course in case of frost.

If it is not possible to take the pipes underground then they could be passed overhead. The connections would have to be in an upstairs room and the pipes boxed in as well as lagged. It would mean that the upstairs central heating flow would need to be a pumped supply; most systems nowadays are pumped anyway but a few are not.

Portable heaters working on paraffin or low pressure gas are easily available and fairly reasonably priced. They give a good heat and also act quickly. There is quite a problem with both types from condensation and for this reason I am not personally in favour of them. I have tried both and so have several other people I know. In each case the idea has been abandoned for this reason. They can be useful in a large workshop where they can be used in conjuction with another, dryer form of heating which will offset the condensation problem. Otherwise they do not seem to be practical proposition. Much the same seems to apply to gas heaters which are run from the main supply.

An old coal or coke stove of the type that used to be used in boats and caravans gives plenty of heat. A chimney will have to be installed in the workshop in order to run one. The chimney need only be a piece of suitable piping and it can either be run through the roof or up the side wall if the building is of concrete or brick. If it is taken through the roof then care must be taken to get a layer of insulation round it where it passes through in case the heat that is generated sets fire to the roof.

One of the modern wood-burning stoves can also be installed in the same way. Some of these are quite cheap and there is a wide range available. This type of heating is certainly efficient and

If a chimney is fitted through the roof there must be a heat shield.

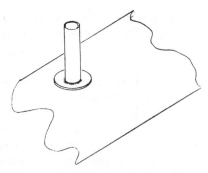

remarkably cosy. It is also possible to use the fire for some model engineering practices such as hardening metal etc. Care must be taken when leaving the workshop that the stove is shut so that sparks cannot fly out and set fire to things.

Finally we come to electricity. A somewhat expensive commodity but, as far as workshop heating is concerned, extremely efficient. If your house is fitted with the economy type meters then a night storage heater is possibly the answer, connected via a suitable time switch. If such a system is not installed it may be better to go for a more direct form of heating.

There is a wide range of electric heaters that can be used. The simple type sold mainly for bathrooms and fitted on the wall is convenient and can be kept out of the way. A fan heater will give a quick warming heat and can be directed to the part of the workshop where it is needed. There are also electric radiators and convector heaters. One type of radiator is oil filled and this can be fairly economical as the heating is thermostatically controlled. Electric heating is a very dry heat and will cause the least condensation and so the least rust.

The Coldwatcher by Dimplex is a 500 watt heater designed to keep greenhouses, sheds etc at a temperature above freezing in the coldest of weather. Taken in conjuction with a well insulated workshop it is a cheap and efficient form of heating.

79

It is desirable if possible to leave some small heating on overnight. This will prevent rapid changes of temperature and so forestall our old enemy rust. The better the workshop is insulated the less the need for overnight heat, but even so some is desirable. There are small heaters available designed for greenhouses that use about a hundred or hundred and fifty watts. These are usually tubular in form. This heat is sufficient in most workshops to keep the condensation off the machines and tools. A recent addition to the market has been a five hundred watt heater. A very small unit, it is quite convenient and will give that little bit of extra heat for the larger workshop. It is thermostatically controlled and so will not be running away with the electricity. An alternative is to use a hundred or hundred and fifty watt light bulb suspended in a tin with ample ventilation. The heat from the bulb ensures the tin getting very warm and makes an efficient form of background heating, certainly sufficient to deal with the rust problem in the small workshop.

It may be that in summer we need to cool the workshop down, I once had a workshop that had a great deal of glass in the construction and it required both winter heating and summer cooling. Open doors and windows will frequently do the trick but they also let out the noise that is created by the machinery etc. A small fan can be a useful item to have in the workshop and these are quite cheap to buy. If a fan heater is used for heating it will usually also have a cool position allowing the fan to be used for cooling purposes. This means only one piece of equipment is needed and so saves space.

No matter what type of heating or cooling is used troubles can be greatly reduced by good insulation. This prevents loss of heat and also entry of it when the days are hot. The ideal workshop I suppose will require neither heat or cooling, relying entirely on its insulation to do both jobs. Alas, it is not a perfect world and so no matter how well we manage to sort the insulation problem out there will be some need to heat the workshop, although with really good insulation it may well remain cool enough for comfort in the summer.

8   SAFETY AND SECURITY

Fire

Fire is a constant risk, whether at home or at work. There is possibly a slight increase in that risk in the workshop. Fires can be caused through bad electrical wiring, overheating of electric motors, hot swarf, and sparks from tools as well as the more obvious risks from careles use of matches etc. The obvious thing is to try to remember not to let fires start rather than how to put them out once they have started. This means taking care, particularly when leaving the workshop after working in it. Check that all gas appliances are turned off, and that electric switches are off. Take plugs out of sockets if possible. The standard electric switch often only switches one pole of the supply off, if there has been a mistake in wiring a plug then there can be a distinct chance of fire occurring through this.

Trying to avoid too many materials in the construction of the workshop that will burn easily is also worthwhile. There will obviously be a need to use wood for many purposes and wood of course is highly inflammable. The risk can be reduced, though, by painting it with emulsion paint rather than gloss. Gloss paints contain oil and are therefore a fire hazard in themselves. Emulsion paints being water based are far more resistant to fires and so are the best type to use. The use of polystyrene too should be avoided if possible. While it makes an excellent insulator it is also highly inflammable and worse still it gives off toxic fumes when burning which can quickly overcome a person in the vicinity. If for any reason its use is essential then paint it with emulsion paint. The styrene absorbs the paint which helps to retard its combustible properties.

Keep flammable liquids such as oil in sealed containers. If a fire does start they will not then help it to spread quite so easily as they would if left open. Do up the the container as soon as you have finished with it. Check that electric motors are not allowed to overheat and do not overload electric sockets; all these help to

A dry powder extinguisher is best for most workshops. This example is 600g, a shade small as 2½kg is recommended.

cause fires. Always clear up the workshop before leaving. The object that causes the fire may be in a pile of swarf or wood shavings and you do not know it is there. It will later burst into flames. One blessing is that you will not be there, but the fire is best prevented.

It is worth thinking of an escape route from the workshop. I have a door at each end of my present one. Prior to that I had a door at one end and a window which I could scramble through at the other. If such arrangements are not possible then have a heavy hammer at the blind end so that you can force your way out if need be. Some means of communication with the house is desirable. A cheap battery operated intercom will do. This can also be useful if you injure yourself and need to get help. Possibly a more important use is to let people know that you are gasping for a cup of tea . . . If a fire does start try to cut off any draughts of air to prevent it spreading.

So much for trying to prevent fires and for escaping should the worst happen. If a fire starts, what can we do about extinguishing it? I have some old blankets in the workshop. These I use to cover machinery not in use. They would also help to smother a small fire if it started. Proper fire blankets can be purchased if you are so inclined. Water is basically not a good medium for workshop fires. It may in the end do more damage than it prevents. Burning oil, for example, will spread everywhere if water is thrown over it. Most fires are possibly started by electrics and water is of no use for those either. Throw on the bucket of water and the result could be a massive electric shock. A bucket of sand is a great deal more use if there is room to keep it. It can also be used for putting work in for small brazing jobs and so serve two purposes.

The obvious thing is to invest in a fire extinguisher. There is a wide variety on the market: some are not all that may be desired so try and get one that conforms to the current British Standard. Do not be tempted to get a very small one. There is probably nothing worse than delaying one's escape only to find that the extinguisher will not put the fire out and you are trapped anyway. There are several types of extinguisher. Some are water filled and while good for general fires have obvious disadvantages in the workshop.

A dry powder extinguisher is probably the best all-round type for our purposes and if possible the extinguisher should be at least 2½ kilogrammes. Anything less might just prove not to have enough in it when the time comes. Keep the appliance in a handy place and make sure you know how to operate it. It is a bit late, when a fire starts, thinking "I must read the instructions if I can find my glasses."

All this may sound somewhat alarmist but it makes sense to be prepared. I have an extinguisher that, touch wood, has never been used, but I am still glad I have it. One final word. Some extinguishers need regular servicing. Make sure this is done if it is needed. Above all as soon as possible call the fire brigade.

Security

Keeping the contents of the workshop secure must be a prime consideration. Although the expenditure on individual items in the workshop may not be very much, when taken as a whole it can be quite astounding what the value is. That thieves can be interested in stealing such equipment there is little doubt, as unfortunately too many people have already discovered.

If the workshop is indoors then the methods used to secure the premises will of course also protect the contents of the workshop. One assumes that the householder will take all possible steps to make the house secure and so there should be no problem. It is with the outside workshop that we are likely to have to think hard about how to stop people entering and helping themselves.

The first thing to think about is access to the garden where the workshop is. Again, if it is in a terraced house with gardens either

The Chubb IK21 Cruiser. Padlock, five lever close shackle case-hardened, off-centre key, shown with vertical bar and hardened steel staple.

side of it and at the back there is little problem, as clambering over garden fences with heavy tooling is unlikely to be resorted to with easier pickings around. However, it is sometimes as well to get to know all the neighbours and whether they are the type of characters that may get involved in such escapades. I think anyway that one of the best forms of security is not to advertise too much the fact that you have a workshop. If nobody knows then garden sheds in terraced houses are certainly not prime targets for burglars.

If there is access to the garden either by a side or rear gate then that is the first place to fortify. It is not easy to do this as climbing a gate or fence and opening it from the inside is not so very difficult. A good heavy bolt will help but it is not by any means the answer. A hasp and padlock on the bolt certainly starts to make life much harder for our would-be visitor. It needs to be a reasonably good padlock, though. Cheap ones can easily be broken open with nothing more than a reasonable sized screwdriver. Still, we are beginning to get some sort of safety as thieves like to work where they cannot be observed and the more time it is going to take to get in then the less they will try. It is also true that a padlock does not stop a thief from climbing the gate to get in. But usually they need to open it to get out and that is where it helps.

It may be worth considering some sort of alarm on the gate, wired in such a way that the alarm bell or siren is concealed away from it. Here we have the situation where the person trying to get in cannot spare the time to try and cut the alarm off for fear of discovery and will beat a hasty retreat.

Having made the access to the ground in which the workshop is

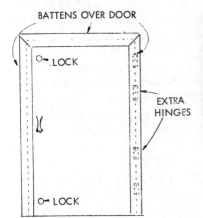

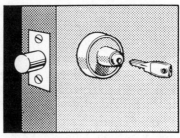

Left, three measures to help make a door more thief-proof. Locks can be of the security bolt type shown above or good quality mortise locks.

situated as secure as possible we must then turn our attention to the workshop itself. The most obvious point of entry is the door. If a prefabricated wooden building has been bought then usually the door is quite a flimsy affair, as it was not designed really for the purpose we have in mind. The first thing that needs to be done is to make it into a double skinned affair with some insulation in between the two layers. This of course also helps retain heat. The inner layer should be of a reasonable quality material and in fact chipboard of say 12mm thickness is quite good. It is extremely difficult stuff to break through and unlike wood will not split if hit with a heavy object. Make sure that the screws that secure it to the door are as long and thick as possible, and do not skimp on the number used.

Hinges can be a weak point. In fact it is frequently the point that is aimed at by the would-be burglar. It might then be a good idea to fit a couple of extra hinges, possibly stronger than those already on the door. I say fit extra rather than replace as one reason that hinges will give way is because of the thief forcing a bow in the door. True, the chipboard will to some extent take care of this but if more hinges are placed along the length of the door then it is almost impossible for the door to bow and so the weak point is eliminated.

Let us now turn our attention to the lock. The usual type of lock fitted to shed doors has a key that enables the door to be opened by any other similar shaped piece of metal. By all means leave it there if you feel so inclined but if possible fit another one or even two. Again one reason locks get pushed in is because the door can be bowed, this time at the opening. A lock top and bottom will prevent this and helps no end in making it secure. Use as good a quality lock as you can. The lock known as the Yale type, more correctly called the rim lock, as made by many firms (in fact Yale make many good security locks but the normal household lock has become known by that name) is not the best for our purposes. Firstly it can be opened easily by a skilled thief. Secondly it can close when you go outside the workshop and lock you out. Unlike the thief you are possibly not very adept at getting the lock open without the key. Use therefore good mortise locks or one of the special security types that are about.

Make sure that the lock is secured to the wood with long screws. It is no good fitting a good lock if the screws that hold it can be pushed out. Probably a better idea is to fit in wall plugs with an epoxy resin adhesive and put the screws in those. The location for the securing bar of the lock needs similar attention. Again there is little point in really well fixing the lock only to allow the door to be pushed open because the part on the door jamb does not hold firm.

The jamb itself can be quite a weak point, particularly in prefabricated wooden sheds. This is no criticism of the manufacturers – it is just that they do not have in mind the specific purpose for which the shed is to be used. What happens if a burglar tries to gain entry is that if a jemmy is put between the door and the jamb then the jamb will bend, allowing the lock to come free. Our lock at top and bottom will help here but it will not completely obviate the trouble. The only real answer is to strengthen the jamb so that it will not bend or bow when levered and this can either be done by screwing angle iron along the full length of it or by fixing wood to it

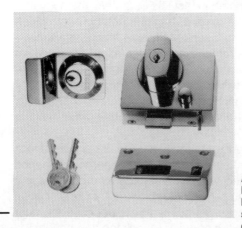

A rim lock by Legge. This has a hardened steel locking bar and an extra-complicated set of tumblers to make it difficult to penetrate.

so that it is effectively at least doubled in size. If wood is to be used then fix it with screws and glue. All wood fixed in position for security reasons should be done in this way. Screws alone can be forced out but with glue as well life is made extremely dificult for the intruder.

Edges of doors should be covered with wooden battens to prevent the insertion of a jemmy or large screwdriver, which is sometimes the tool used. Again, our prefabricated wooden shed is frequently not strong enough at these points. If there is already some beading or battening round the door then make sure it is glued and not just nailed in position. There is nothing easier than pulling nailed wood away from the point to which it is nailed. Battening round the door of course also helps with draught proofing and so will serve two purposes.

Having dealt with the door then the next obvious place to worry about is the window or windows. Strengthening round the frames is always worth thinking about. Double glazing makes life difficult for the thief, and in particular it does so if the secondary glazing is of good quality plastic. Plastic can be extremely difficult stuff to break and is possibly better than glass as a deterrent. All opening windows should be fitted with some form of safety lock. These are cheap to buy or easy to make. All that is required to make one is a piece of mild steel plate and a similar sized piece of mild steel angle. Drill four screw holes, two in each piece. Drill through the angle and the plate, and tap the hole in the plate. Screw it up with an allen headed screw and you have as good a safety device for an opening window as it is possible to get.

One further suggestion on windows is to fit wooden shutters Anyone who has travelled on the continent will know that these make life very difficult indeed for the thief. They can be made to fasten back when the workshop is in use and can be secured on the inside with a steel bar. It does mean that the window itself will have to be made so that it can be secured after the shutters but this should not be too much of a problem. The alternative is to make the shutters so that they do up on the outside using something like the allen headed screw again. It is highly unlikely that the would-be thief will be carrying a selection of allen keys around with him or her.

Having made the place as secure as possible we should possibly turn our attention to some sort of alarm. These come in a variety of types and work in various ways. The output will either be from a siren or a bell but it is the operation that concerns us. A good method is a pressure pad under a mat by the door. When the

Superswitch make this alarm system. It is shown here in full view but when installed should be concealed. An infra red beam triggers the alarm when someone breaks it.

intruder steps on the mat the alarm is triggered. It can be operated on a very low voltage system and this can be supplied by batteries. If fitting such a system then it is a good idea to have a lock-on type of relay so that once the alarm is set off it will not stop if the intruder gets off the mat.

There is a whole variety of other types of alarms available. Some work simply when a door or window is opened. Others have sensors and react to a person getting near the premises. Some also switch on lights. The best idea is to contact a supplier and get advice.

That takes care of the workshop in the garden as far as it is possible to do so on paper. The other one that is vulnerable is the workshop in a garage. Basically all the advice given relating to the outside workshop applies, particularly as far as alarms etc. are concerned. If the workshop section is partitioned from the rest of the garage then make sure that locks are fitted to the communicating door. If you are likely to leave the workshop by the rear entrance then an ordinary bolt top and bottom is the best form of security for the connecting door, if not then again all that was said about locks on the shed door applies.

The garage door itself is a problem. The very size of it makes securing it difficult. Opening doors are very flexible and easily forced. A good bolt top and bottom on the one side and a strengthening strip up the side that opens on the lock will help, as will the idea of a lock top and bottom.

Up and over doors need to be looked at carefully. There are many different types and each will need to be dealt with in its own way. The usual weak spot is the latch at the top of the door. An

Recommended use of a standard simple security bolt at four rather vulnerable points. You get what you pay for in overall strength, bolt hardness and complexity of tumblers.

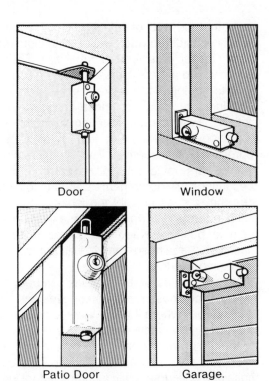

Door

Window

Patio Door

Garage.

instrument pushed in the gap can free this even if it is locked and allow unauthorised entry. A wooden batten along the top will prevent this, and even better would be to reinforce it with a piece of angle iron. There is no reason why an alarm should not be fitted to the garage door and this is possibly the best form of defence. The one trouble with a workshop inside a garage is that once the intruder gets into the garage itself he or she is out of sight and can then take as long as is wanted to get into the workshop itself. The answer must be to prevent entry to the garage if possible.

The final piece of advice is if in doubt contact your local police station. The Crime Prevention Officer is trained to know the best device for the particular situation and will offer you advice on the best way to go about things. He will even pay a visit if it is likely to help.

Safety

Safety precautions in the home workshop are sensible, even though they may seem to be somewhat irksome. Where possible guards should be on machines when they are operated, and most certainly all belts should have guards over them. There is no doubt that the level of safety precaution in the home workshop is usually considerably below that in an industrial building where the factory inspector is likely to pay a visit. There is no compulsion in law for you to protect yourself providing there is no one else that is likely to get injured. It makes sense to do so, though.

In industry there is, these days, an accent on protective clothing. Most people working at home want to go into the workshop and relax, not first of all dress up as something representing a spaceman. This is understandable and indeed the feelings are mine too. However, one or two easy, sensible precautions will do no harm. Let us take clothing first. Just make sure the sleeves are not too loose round the cuffs so they can catch in the work. If they are loose then an elastic band will keep them in position. Keep the overall done up when using any machinery, again so that it will not catch up in a chuck or something like that.

Wearing protective eye-shields can be a nuisance. We cannot, however, purchase replacement eyes and so it is as well to wear them for jobs where there is likely to be some danger to the eyes. Some are remarkably cheap to buy and it is worth hanging a pair by the lathe and perhaps one by the vice and slipping them on when you are using either of these. The same applies to other machines of course. Only a complete fool would fail to wear them when using a grinding machine with the danger of grit coming up and getting in the eye, or worse still the wheel shattering and injuring you in that way. If safety glasses are found to be too uncomfortable complete head shields are available and these I find much more comfortable to wear.

Masks should be worn when carrying out jobs where a lot of dust is generated or where there are likely to be toxic fumes. Again grinding is a good example of a dust-generating operation and brazing or silver soldering can generate fumes that will give rise to sore throats and headaches. Once more no one is suggesting that the whole time in the workshop should be spent wearing a face mask but they are well worthwhile in the sort of instances quoted. There is a wide variety on the market, many are quite cheap and one to your liking is sure to be found.

For welding then the correct type of goggles must be worn. If arc welding a full face mask or shield is essential. These operations can permanently damage the eyesight. Arc welding in particular can be very dangerous and anyone in the workshop with you when such an operation is carried out should also have a suitable shield or mask. This is to prevent the dangerous light emitted by the welding from damaging the eyes.

Do not be tempted to wear carpet slippers in the workshop. Heavy shoes are needed. A large piece of metal falling from the bench on to the toes can cause an exclamation of annoyance. There is also the possibility of treading on a sharp object or even dropping something hot on the foot. Some sort of protection is needed. Again it is probably not necessary to go to the extent of using an industrial boot, but certainly shoes should be worn at all times.

Badly maintained tools can be a cause of accidents. Make sure that chisel shafts are not mushroomed out at the top. Check that hammer heads are secure, and do not leave sharp edged tools lying about in drawers to cut the exploring hand. Any liquids spilt on the workshop floor should be cleaned up at once to prevent slipping. Swarf too can be a potential hazard and should be cleaned off a machine as soon as possible.

Do not leave keys in chucks, it is all too easy to forget they are there. Also do not put metal in a chuck or vice without tightening up. If something happens to distract you, when returning to the work it may be thought that the work is secure, and the machine started up with painful results.

This all sounds as though our workshop activities are becoming a bit of a bore but this is not really so. It is just a case of taking a few simple precautions in order to enjoy ourselves the better.

9   LATHES

For the model engineer or the clockmaker a lathe is essential and for many other forms of modelling it is highly desirable. Making a decision on what lathe to fit the workshop with is not going to be that easy because of the wide diversity of machines available. They range from little tiny models like the Unimat 1, which is made from high impact plastic but for all of that it can be used for small work quite successfully. We then come to the next range which include lathes such as the Peatol, Cowells, Toyo and Unimat 3, plus quite a few others which are worth consideration. These lathes are quite capable of doing a useful job of work and if there is no space for anything else then any of them is well worth having. They are ideal for the clockmaker, as well as being suitable as second machines for those fortunate enough to have both space and cash for such a thing. In this case they can be

Cowells are a British firm specialising in small machines. This is one of their range of small lathes.

The Toyo lathes come from Japan. This is the 210, a high precision machine and a milling attachment is obtainable for use with it.

used for those awkward little parts that are not so easy to make on a bigger lathe.

The next range up includes such machines as the Toyo 360, the Myford ML10 and the Emco Compact 5. We are now getting to the point where the lathe is capable of doing quite large work and this size of lathe is used by many modellers.

Probably the most popular size of machine is the slightly larger one such as the Myford 7 series and the Emco 8. Here we are getting into the range of machines that will be capable of virtually anything that most modellers are likely to ask of them. Once again there are many such machines on the market, including these

The 918 model engineer's lathe by Warren Machine Tools. This is a large rugged machine at a competitive price.

British manufacturers Boxford, best known for industrial machinery, do produce the MEIO especially for model engineers. Available direct from the factory.

days quite a number of cheap imports. Although these cheaper lathes look rather rough some are very good and, if cash is a problem, well worth thinking about.

Also available and yet still suitable for the model engineer is a range of slightly larger machines. The Myford 254s, and Emco 10 immediately spring to mind, but there are many more and again there are are some fairly cheap imported machines that might be worth consideration.

Second-hand machines of all shapes and sizes are invariably available either by buying direct from the owner or through one of

Bigger brother of the Austrian Unimat is the Emco Compact 5, a nice little machine of good quality.

the specialist second-hand dealers. They are also frequently sold at auctions and this can be a good way of obtaining a cheap lathe. There are two types of auctions to keep one's eyes open for, the regular machinery sale and the local one. The prices at regular machinery sales tend to be rather higher as it is to those that people looking for machinery gravitate. Local auctions can be quite fascinating. Frequently a small engineering workshop will be put up for sale and combined by the auctioneer with other items. These can be almost any type of goods. It is more than possible that the majority of people attending the auction will be doing so to purchase the main sale items and not the workshop equipment,

The Myford Super 7 lathe, the most popular among model engineers and also found in innumerable light industrial workshops.

the result being that it goes at what can only be described as knock-down prices.

It is as well to have some idea what to look for when buying a second-hand lathe. Condition is obviously a good guide and if the history of the machine is known then that will be a help. Personally I would tend to avoid machines from secondary schools which often have been used to their limit and are not always as well maintained as they might be. Find out too what the motor is. If you only have single phase electricity then a three phase motor is not a good buy unless you are capable of carrying out the required conversions yourself.

Having obtained your precious lathe thought must be given as to where it is to be sited in the workshop. It will need a sound support and either a commercial stand or a home-built bench will do. If a bench is to be built then it should if at all possible be made of steel rather than wood, which is inclined to warp. It should be bolted to the wall as well as to the floor if possible and some form of tray is desirable to catch swarf, oil etc. This advice is mainly aimed of course at those obtaining the larger lathes. Fortunately the smaller ones can be picked up and put down as required.

Whether or not the lathe should be sited near a window is an interesting point. It is nice to have natural light available if possible, but if the lathe is placed wrongly then that natural light could be coming from the back and this is not a good thing. It is desirable, if it can be done, to get a window at one end. It a second window can also be sited at the rear of the lathe, although it means the light coming from the back there are advantages in having a window in that situation, particularly if it opens. This will enable the machine to be cleaned at the back much more easily than could be done otherwise. I also know of one modeller who has used an open window in that position to mount extra long work on the cross-slide.

A window at the headstock end has advantages for the same reason. It is possible to put long bars of metal into the mandrel by

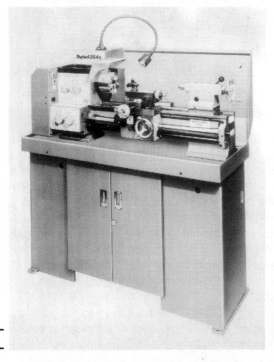

The Myford 254s is the latest in the Myford range for the model engineer. Highly sophisticated, it is nevertheless proving very popular.

feeding them through the open window. Certainly, whatever happens do not put the lathe too near a wall at the headstock end as metal will have to be put in through the mandrel from time to time and space will be required. At the other end there must be room to remove the tailstock as required.

The electrical point from which the machine will be operated is dealt with under the chapter on electricity. Even so, remember that long trailing wires are a hazard in the workshop and so put the lathe near an outlet socket if possible.

If you are at all doubtful about your competence in buying a lathe then get as many brochures as possible and get hold of some books on the subject and read up what to look for if buying a lathe. Make sure what equipment will come with the lathe. It is no good thinking that so and so model is a bargain if when it finally arrives there are no chucks and no motor. Make sure that there is sufficient equipment for the lathe to be used by you for what you want to do with it. Again reading up on the subject will help.

10   MILLING MACHINES

For the model engineer a milling machine is desirable, although not absolutely necessary. Many fine models have been made without the use of such a machine, and we use instead a tool called a vertical slide. This bolts to the lathe cross-slide and allows work that is clamped to it to move up and down as well as being able to travel with the cross-slide. With a milling cutter held in the lathe chuck we have what amounts to a milling machine laid on its side.

If we come to milling machines as a separate item, then there is a wide choice available. This was not always so, but nowadays such a machine is becoming more and more a feature of the model engineer's workshop. The most popular type is the vertical

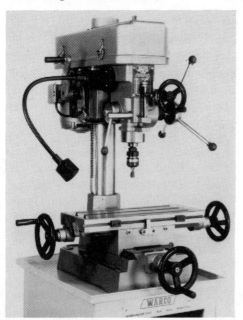

Possibly the most popular type of milling machine is the mill drill. As the name suggests it can be used either for drilling or milling. A range of three sizes is available. The machine is seen here mounted on a stand. Photograph courtesy of Warren Machine Tools.

The Sharp Mk.2 by Town Bent Engineering converts from vertical to horizontal milling. A compact machine, it can cope with quite large work.

one which sometimes can be converted very quickly to a drilling machine. It is also possible to purchase a drilling machine that converts for milling.

The range of sizes available in vertical milling machines is quite large. It is going to be a compromise between what can be afforded, and how much room is available, plus of course what size is likely to be needed for present and future projects. It is as well to buy one as large as possible as a rule. In some cases, however, such a machine would be far too clumsy and a small machine would easily be the best type for some individuals.

A horizontal milling machine is possibly of limited use to most model makers. The form of its construction means that large heavy cuts can be taken from metal in comparison to the vertical miller. It will not always do jobs that the model engineer requires as well as the vertical type. Even so it has the advantage of rigidity if work is to be carried out on heavy material where large area cutting is required.

The universal milling machine comes in two types these days, the vertical miller with a swivelling head which is often referred to as a turret milling machine, and the true universal which can be converted into either a horizontal or a vertical machine. Here of course we have the best of both worlds, but like all things one gets what one pays for and so a universal machine is going to work out much more expensive.

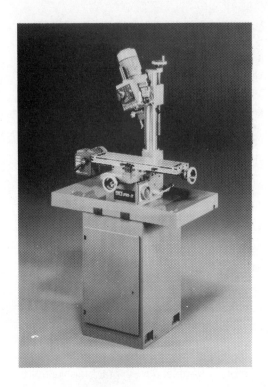

The Emco FB2 is a nice, medium size vertical miller (seen here on a stand but available for bench mounting). Excellent for a small workshop.

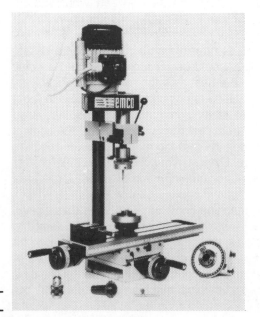

The Emco Compact 5 milling machine consists of a column, a head and a compound slide. Can be obtained for fitting to the Compact 5 lathe.

The very small machines come for bench mounting. Larger ones usually have specially made stands as an extra. Sometimes just the tray part of the stand can be purchased. If a very large machine is purchased then a stand will be part of it. Such machines would require benches of massive proportions to withstand the weight as milling machines are extremely heavy. Personally I feel that if there is room for a stand in the workshop then it is worth the investment. A milling machine when in use causes a great deal of vibration and if it is bench mounted then that vibration will shake tools lying on the bench all over the place. Whether a stand is used or not a tray is certainly most desirable. The machine creates a lot of swarf and also requires the use of a cutting oil and this will all go on to the bench unless there is a suitable tray to catch it.

Apart from the wide range of machines that can be purchased new, there is also a good second-hand market. Such machines are often advertised privately and they are also available from dealers who specialise in second-hand machinery. Many milling machines sold off by industry are three phase and so care will have to be taken when making a selection that the machine is suitable for the electricity supply that is available.

Most machines when sold, whether new or second-hand, are likely to be supplied without the facilities for holding a milling

Ted Jolliffe bought this big and heavy turret mill second-hand at a very good price; damaged table is not difficult to repair.

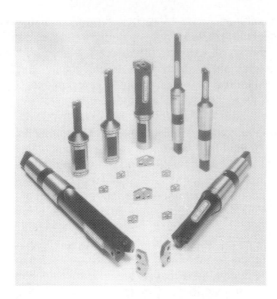

A selection of end mills by Stellram. These have carbide tips which are replaced and save the need for sharpening.

cutter. Enquiries should be made when purchasing to establish what type of device is required (usually some form of collet). These devices are expensive and will add to the cost of the machine and this cost must be considered. Also ensure that the device is still available, as occasionally milling machines are sold off and the cutter holders have become obsolete. The machines can be adapted for other means of holding but this is not so easy as all that.

Other accessories that will be required when a milling machine is purchased are cutters and various vices for holding work on the machine. There is a range of such cutters and the best idea is to consult a good tool catalogue to decide what is required. For a vertical milling machine then basic work can be carried out with either end mills or slot drills. These are similar tools but the end mill has four flutes and the slot cutter two. End mills are also available in a three fluted version as well. Variations on the end mill include tee slot cutters and dovetail cutters of various angles as well as some radiusing types. For the horizontal milling machine either an ordinary face cutter or a side and face type is the most common. Thin slitting saws can be used on both machines, but for the vertical miller a special arbor would need to be made up to hold the saw.

Sharpening milling cutters is a problem. Special machines that grind the correct angles are required. There are several designs available to enable these to be made at home but they involve

For creating curves on a milling machine a rotary table is needed. This one from Warren Machine Tools, can be used as shown or laid flat and is available in sizes from 6 to 14in. dia.

considerable work. Throw-away end mills can be obtained and when they are blunted they are designed to be disposed of. For this reason they are correspondingly cheaper than the normal type. It is also possible to purchase tools with replaceable carbide blades, or tips as they are often called. These make it easy to keep sharp tools available. Such tips do not like heavy shocks and therefore they must be used with care to avoid unnecessary breakages.

Machine vices are available in many sizes and they can also be obtained in tilting versions which enable angles to be cut. The bigger the vice the more rigid it is as a rule, but the choice must be made by the individual. It is sometimes a good idea to get two identical vices. This will allow long work to be held without any overhang at the ends.

There are of course many other accessories that can be obtained to increase the versatility of the machine. It is not really part of the function of this book to suggest such things and the reader must look for information elsewhere. It may be as well, though, to mention the rotary table. This enables radii to be cut and also allows divisions to be made on work. Again a wide range is on the market both new and second-hand, as well as various kits for making them.

11   DRILLING MACHINES

Most work required by the model engineer can be carried out on the lathe. It is a surprisingly adaptable machine and is capable of being used for all sorts of different purposes. Once again I would suggest that those readers who do not know how to get the best from their lathes get hold of a good book and read it thoroughly. Make sure, though, that the book is one aimed at the model engineer, as technical books for students describe the use of a lathe as a lathe and not as a jack of all trades.

The first most obvious machine other than a lathe in which the model engineer will be interested is a driling machine. Once again we have a market that is absolutely flooded with suitable models. It will have to be decided what sort of machine is required and what it is expected to do. For those making smaller models there

The simplest form of bench drill is a hand drill on a stand. There are quite a few modellers who use this system with complete success.

A bench drill from Emco. This is a good solid model with a large table and is designed to be screwed to the bench. Note transparent guard in operating area, an attachment increasingly included nowadays.

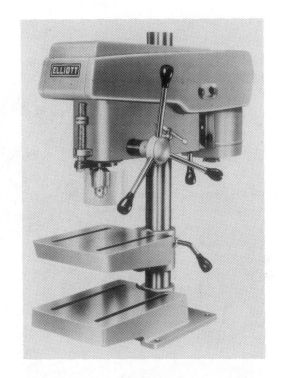

This bench drill from Warren Machine Tools has a rack-operated table which is also designed to revolve. The drill is meant to be free standing on a bench and has a capacity of up to 1in. dia. drills. Can also be supplied as a floor-standing model.

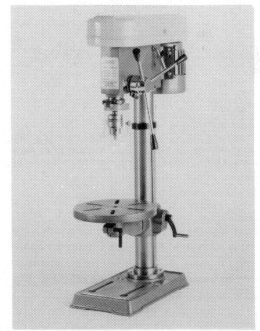

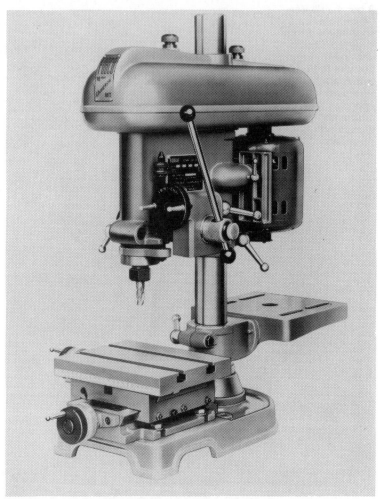

The Fobco Universal Drilling Machine has a tilting table and Morse taper spindle to accept large drills. Smaller drills are accommodated in the chuck shown inset. A favourite tool for model engineers.

are several very good machines with a capacity of ¼ in. or 6mm. This relates to the size of drill that can be accommodated. For very many people this will be sufficient.

For those wishing to buy a machine with a larger capacity there are models with capacities of ⅜ in. – 10mm or ½ in. – 12mm. These will cope with most things the model engineer needs. Take

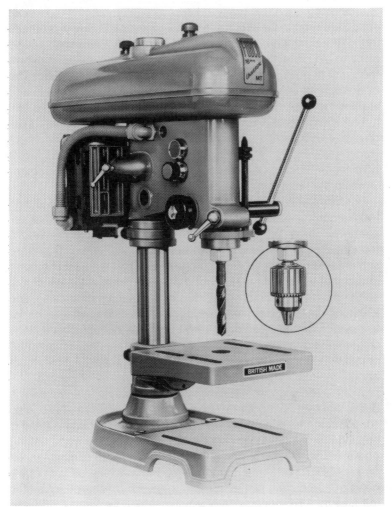

The Fobco in use as a mill. A milling cutter has been fitted to the Morse taper and the table has been swung away to enable a small milling table to be fitted. Cutter feed control near drilling handle.

care that the motor has sufficient capacity to drive the size of drill. Some Far Eastern imported models have the larger chuck fitted to a machine meant for a smaller one. The result is that the motor has difficulty coping with, say, a ½ in. drill. The motor should be at least ¼ horse power for that size.

Drilling machines come as either bench-mounted or floor-standing models. You really take your choice as to which most suits the purpose for which it is required. If space is at a premium then the bench-mounted version allows storage space underneath. The floor-standing model, however, usually allows the swarf to go straight to the floor where it is easily swept up. The bench type often means that swarf gets tangled up with tools and work. When I started this book I went round to many people and asked them about their workshops. I also asked for any suggestions that would help readers. I always remember Brent Hudson saying that a drilling machine must be isolated as far as possible in order to prevent swarf becoming entangled with other items in the workshop. It is certainly sound advice.

For those with larger ambitions drilling machines are available with larger capacities than those mentioned. Prices tend to get somewhat high as size increases. The drilling table is worth a thought. Here again we have a whole variety of types. There are some round ones that will rotate and others that will not. There are tables that will tilt. Have a good look round and decide which will suit best. It is possible on all the larger machines to raise and lower the drilling table. It may be as well to consider whether or not to buy one that has a rack system to do this. With heavy castings or something similar fixed to a table which has to be moved up and down there can be problems if it is lifted by hand. A rack with a handle makes life very much easier for the operator.

Work for drilling will require securing to the table otherwise if it is being held by hand there is a danger of injury. There also sometimes arises the problem of a drill jamming and one hand is holding the drill down while the other is holding the work. Letting go will cause the drill to break in the work. In these circumstances one usually resorts to trying to switch the machine off with one's head or some such similar idea. If the work is secured a hand is left free for emergencies. A special vice can be used and these are dealt with in the section referring to vices.

For those whose cash is too limited to think about a new machine there is a lively second-hand market. A good alternative can be a vertical stand for the ordinary DIY type of electric drill, but a better idea is to get some castings and to make a drilling machine.This is far from being as difficult as it sounds and many model engineering suppliers keep castings and drawings for this purpose. Sales of these are high so there must be plenty of people who do make their own machines.

12   SAWS AND GRINDERS

Whatever hobby we are proposing to carry out in our workshop we will need to cut some sort of material. For this we will need suitable tools or machines. It would not be possible to go through every possible hobby and suggest the right tools, and indeed I do not think I have sufficient knowledge of some hobbies to offer guidance to people on the tools to use. Someone who is going to do bookbinding, for example, needs a method of cutting thick wads of paper perfectly square, while someone interested in photography needs a guillotine to trim the photographs. I propose then to deal in this chapter with tools for the model engineer and elsewhere with those for the woodworker. No doubt those

A small power hacksaw by Blackgates Engineering. Bench mounted, it is designed to take standard hacksaw blades. Larger models are usually floor-standing and have special blades.

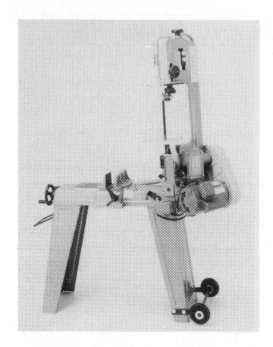

A vertical/horizontal band saw from Warren Machine Tools. The arm with the blade comes down to the horizontal position for cutting off lengths of metal bar. In the upright position the tool can be used as a band saw.

engaged in other hobbies will either know what equipment they require or find what they want among the things suggested here.

The main need of the model engineer is for something with which to cut metal. I hardly need tell readers that we use a

The Emco band saw. A useful tool for cutting metal that is not too heavy. It is capable of cutting shapes as well as straight. Guides are supplied for cutting at various angles and a small emery wheel is fitted on ther side of the casing.

hacksaw for this. There are large hacksaws and small ones, the latter usually referred to as junior hacksaws. The choice must remain with the individual, but it is possibly as well to get one of each. As the saw will be used in conjunction with the vice then the storage space for it should be near to the vice. For those more awkward jobs a coping saw or piercing saw can be used and these too can be stored near the vice.

Cutting metal can be hard work and the idea of a hobby is relaxation. It might then be a good idea to consider some form of mechanical sawing device, of which there is a wide range. For just cutting straight across metal bars then a power hacksaw of the reciprocating type is worth consideration. These are really only an ordinary hacksaw arranged to work in a straight line and motorised. They can be made quite easily or can be purchased. Some will mount on a bench, others need a floor space on which to stand.

Bandsaws will cut metal both straight and to shapes – sometimes to shapes when not required to do so! With careful use they are a good buy and I have used one for many years to cut metal of all types, as well as a variety of other materials, all of varying thicknesses. As usual, bandsaws range from comparatively inexpensive tools to much more sophisticated ones. The bandsaw works with a prepared saw blade that is formed into a complete band. It runs round either two or three large wheels and metal is pushed against it as it rotates. Some of the smaller ones will mount on a bench. They are used with the blade in the vertical

A close-up view of the blade of a Cowells jigsaw. The blade slides in a groove in the piece of rod and does not rely on a spring frame to tension it.

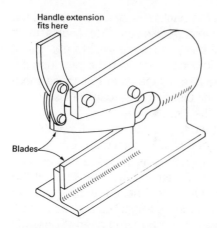

Handle extension
fits here

Blades

A small guillotine is a useful machine for cutting heavier sheet metal. Can be bench-mounted or gripped in a vice.

position and this enables the operator to see the work being carried out.

More recently bandsaws have been introduced that can be used either vertically or horizontally. Combined with a vice this enables heavy metal section to be clamped to the machine and left while the machine takes care of the cutting. In the upright position they can be used as a bandsaw but are limited to the

A trio of bench grinders ranging in size from 5 to 8 inch wheels from Warren. Note built in eye guards and tool rests.

radius that can be cut because of the wider blade used on this type compared with the normal bandsaw.

Bandsaws are made with either two or three wheels for the blade to run on, the three-wheel type giving a greater clearance to the length of work that can be pushed underneath. The two-wheel type without doubt is a far more accurate machine, even if the size is more limited. Although it is not possible to get such long work under the two-wheel type because of the clearances, the machines will cut thicker material than will the three-wheel models.

There are other types of saws available for metal cutting. The radial type saw with a circular blade is one that immediately springs to mind. They are very good but rather expensive to buy and will only make straight cuts across a limited size of metal. They are really designed for use in industry where the operator needs to be constantly trimming metal of a limited thickness to size. In the same category we have devices which use a thin grinding wheel in a similar way and the same general comments apply.

Grinders

Some form of grindstone is essential if lathe tools and drills are to be used. The usual type of machine consists of two wheels of different textures on a common shaft, which is part of an electric motor. Some form of cover is partially over the grinding wheels and there is almost certain to be a rest to support the tool while it is being ground. Both size and quality will depend on what is paid for the machine. Where possible the larger sizes are worth having, as not only is it easier to see what is happening when they are used but the wheels have a longer life before becoming mis-shapen.

All grinding materials consist of some form of crushed stone held together with an adhesive compound. This can either be spread on cloth or paper to form one of the various abrasive cloths and papers available, or made into belts. A further option is for the mixture to be moulded into grinding wheels. How coarse the abrasive depends on what the material is, how finely it has been crushed and its density. There are tables to deal with this and a code on the paper washer of the grinding wheel gives details of the make-up. Normally, however, abrasives are ordered as very fine, fine, medium, coarse and extra coarse. For most purposes this information is sufficient and I do not propose to give a mass of details of the various grinding substances and their numbers.

The abrasives wear because the crushed material is dislodged piece by piece from the compound which binds it. In the case of a

Few amateur or small workshops would aspire to a drill sharpening machine such as this pedestal-mounted Adko. Note sharpening guide and tub for cooling water.

grinding wheel the wear will take the form of hollows and grooves. Special tools can be purchased that can be run over the stones to restore their shape. These usually consist of a diamond in a holder, and being very hard it rapidly wears away the rest of the stone around the groove and so the shape can be restored.

All grinding operations, whether with a grindstone or with a belt sanding device, or indeed even with a humble piece of emery cloth, leave behind a residue of the abrasive material. Remember it is not the abrasive that wears away but the compound with which it is mixed. In the case of the belt sander and the grindstone this can be carried through the air for quite some distance. Being very abrasive it is likely to cause wear on anything upon which it settles and this includes your machinery. Every effort therefore should be made to put such machines as far away from other machinery as possible. This of course goes against the preaching I have stressed all along, about having related objects near to each other, but this is different, and everything that can be done to stop abrasive dust getting on a machine should be. Not only should the grinder be put as far away as possible but if it can be arranged some sort of shield should be built to catch at least some of the dust that is generated.

A wet-stone grinder used for grinding woodworking tools. The large wheel rotates slowly half submerged in water. This prevents the tools from overheating and prevents harmful dust from flying about.

From time to time the grinding wheels will need to be changed on the grinding machine. All new wheels have a paper washer on them: do not remove this, as it is part of the strength of the wheel. It also gives valuable information about the wheel such as the coarseness and the maximum speed at which it can be used. This latter piece of information is very important as the speed shown on the wheel must under no circumstances be exceeded. The construction of grinding wheels is such that they are designed to stay in one piece up to a certain speed. Beyond that they can and will disintegrate. A wheel which does this is extremely dangerous and when it explodes (that is exactly what it does) the pieces fly everywhere with great force. So make sure of the maximum speed and the speed of your machine before fitting a new wheel.

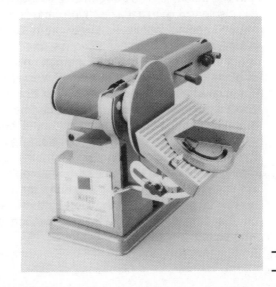

A combined belt and disc sander from Warren Machine Tools. A useful tool but one that produces a lot of dust.

115

A simple drill grinding jig for small drills. This is made from a metal block and enables the user to get the correct angle on the drill.

All grinding wheels should be fitted with large washers on either side, to support the wheel. If pressure is put on one side of it when it is rotating then the forces imposed are tremendous. Remember it is only glued together and so if too much pressure is applied at the side it will break up or explode. The large washers increase the area of support and so decrease the possibility of the wheel disintegrating. In operation it is advisable to use only the periphery of the wheel anyway.

Belt sanding machines are becoming quite popular these days. They can save a lot of filing, and can be obtained with various belt thicknesses and either as a separate machine or attached to a grinding machine. The belt can be either vertical or horizontal, and it is also possible to get a disc type sanding machine. The remarks about keeping abrasives away from other machinery apply equally to these machines as to the grinders.

For those who find difficulty sharpening tools without some form of guide then there are a number of aids such as drill sharpening jigs available. For sharpening milling cutters and similar tools a special machine is needed. These can be made from parts that are obtainable from the various model engineering suppliers. They can also be purchased, but doing this is very expensive. One answer to the tool sharpening problem, whether lathe tools or milling cutters, is to use specially made tools with carbide tips that are screwed into position. The tips are thrown away after use and new ones fitted. The finish given by these tools is exceptionally good and they are well worth consideration, particularly for those who cannot sharpen their own tools.

13 MAKING TOOLS: ELECTRIC MOTORS

Make or Buy

To stock a workshop quickly the obvious thing, if funds are available, is to go out to the various suppliers and to buy exactly what is needed. This does not have to be done at one go and can take a period of many years. Most of the needs of model engineers are available at stockists, although my opinion is that there are many desirable items that cannot be purchased. Sometimes of course we need something that cannot be afforded in order to make a particular model and this can make life difficult, to say the least. The alternative is to make things rather than buy them. Not only does one acquire what is needed in this way but the tool or device is tailor made for the workshop. There is of course a considerable cash saving, but making things takes up valuable modelling time. It may be as well to compromise and to make what we need but cannot immediately afford, and also to

A useful device to make at home that would otherwise be very expensive is a boring head. This one, for use on either a lathe or a milling machine, is available as a kit from Woking Precision Models.

An interesting device for anyone thinking of making a small milling machine is this compound table for home construction by Reeves. To avoid the most difficult bit Myford leadscrews, easily obtained as spares, are used.

Rotary tables are expensive to buy. There are various kits available; this is a neat little one that can be made on most small lathes and is fully geared. The kit of parts is by Hemmingway.

make those things that cannot be bought anyway. There is a tremendous feeling of pride in using a tool made by one's own efforts and this in itself may be sufficient justification for the time that was spent on it.

Just about everything that can be bought can be made, the only

A simple item well worth making is an angle plate. This one, made by the author, was from a casting by College Engineering Supplies.

difficulty being the equipment to make it with. But these things tend to be self-generating and making one thing enables another to be made at a later date. I do not intend to list tools and equipment for the reader to make as they must be an individual choice, but I do however include a series of photographs of equipment which can either be completely fabricated or for which castings are available from one or other of the suppliers.

Electric Motors

Having stressed the idea of both making one's own workshop equipment and possibly buying second-hand machinery, I thought that a word or two on the type of electric motor likely to be needed to run these things would not come amiss.

There are a great many motors on the market and there is also a lively second-hand market in them. The most obvious need on which to satisfy oneself when buying a motor, whether new or second-hand, is that it is designed to work at the correct voltage. This may sound rather obvious but there have been many cases of motors bought that were not correct. The second thing one needs to know is whether or not it will have the power to do the job. It is hard to give a ruling on what is enough power. The average 3 inch centre height lathe needs a motor of at least half a horse power, a small milling machine a quarter horse power or more, and a mechanical saw needs a similar amount of power. A bench grinder or a cutter grinder needs about one sixth of a horse power. These figures are only approximate but they are a reasonable guide.

If buying a second-hand motor then an obvious thing is to ensure that it works. Not just that it will start up but that it will run under some sort of load for a period of time without undue heating up. Most motors do run quite hot, but if you smell burning then you could have trouble. Check that the casing has not rusted away and that the terminals are in good order without a lot of frayed wire attached to them.

The motor if it has to be reversed will need to have four terminals. This does not mean that a motor with three terminals cannot be reversed – it probably can, but it could be a great deal more complicated to do so. Four terminals are of course to be preferred when a new motor is purchased if it is to be reversed, unless you or someone you know is capable of carrying out the necessary conversation.

Shaded pole motors will run very hot and frequently run in the reverse direction to that which we require. Reversing them is

A foot-mounted motor is probably the most useful and commonest type in the average workshop. (Courtesy V.J. Cox).

possible but it means completely dismantling the motor and re-assembling it end for end in relation to the stator. They will not run on D/C current. Shaded pole motors are frequently found in old washing machines. In fact all old washing machine motors should be treated with caution if considering purchasing one. This is not to say that they cannot be a very good buy indeed, as they are often obtainable very cheaply. It is just that when purchasing such a motor enquiries should first of all be made to ensure that it will do the job for which it is required.

Series wound motors are also commonly available on the second-hand market. They are not really suitable for the purposes we have in mind.

If buying second-hand machinery then often it will be fitted with a three phase motor. Household electricity is single phase. Now it is possible to run a three phase motor on single phase electricity and in fact there have been articles and books written on the subject of how to do so. If one is considering the use of three

The internals of an induction motor. This and the illustration above are from *Electric Motors* in the Argus Workshop Practice series.

phase motors it might be as well to invest in a three phase converter. This is a device that will change the current in your workshop into three phase. Such converters are easy to obtain and to fit and can repay their cost in the savings made when purchasing machinery, as well as in the extra efficiency gained from the use of three phase motors.

Looking at three phase electricity in the very briefest of terms we are looking at a system where there is an extra positive current. We therefore have three wires plus an earth rather than the normal two. This extra wiring allows for much easier starting of electric motors. Particularly in the case of large motors a great deal of energy is needed in the starting and the three phase current eases this. It becomes obvious though that other types of fittings are required than the normal household ones.

Because of this heavy starting current single phase motors of a quarter horsepower or over should always be fitted with a capacitor. This absorbs the shock that would otherwise blow the fuses. Motors should always be wired through a proper starting switch with an overload protection. If the motor is switched on and off via an ordinary household switch there is a possibility that after a while the terminals will either burn away or weld themselves together.

There is no doubt that the correct selection of an electric motor is essential and so to sum up, for working on the ordinary single phase household electricity supply purchase a reasonable motor with a capacitor start. If it is to be reversed get one with four terminals and you will not go far wrong. If you have any real problems then look up your local electric motor repair agent in the yellow pages. I have always found them very helpful and often they have spare motors that they will sell at a reasonable price.

14 WOODWORKING

There is not a great deal of difference in the workshop required by the woodworker to that needed by the model engineer, apart from the stocking of it. The woodworker will need to store bulkier but lighter material. He or she will possibly need less tool space as the very wide variety of tools needed by the engineer is not reflected in the work of the woodworker. The bench and vice will also differ. If there is room it is a good idea for anyone indulging in this hobby to have two benches of identical height and width, spaced a little way apart. This will allow for working on very long lengths of timber.

In both the case of the metal worker and that of the woodworker good ventilation is essential. For the metal worker it is to get rid of toxic fumes. This could also apply to the woodworker using some wood treatments. Most important is the need to get rid of dust. Wood dust tends to fly all over the place and can be very uncomfortable. If some sort of extractor can be fitted up so well and good. A lot of modern machinery is already fitted with dust extractors and suitable bags for containing it, and whilst this may cost a little more the investment is well worth while.

The storage of hand tools is often taken care of in woodworking by using the bench ends, to which racks are fitted. Chisels should

The Emco TS 5 circular saw. A machine like this will cut far more accurately than is possible with a handsaw.

The Alko 5005 Multiworker in use as a planer. Among many other guises it is a useful saw and even has a flexible shaft attachment.

always be kept in racks to prevent them losing their sharpness, and having the rack on the bench means that they are close to where they will be needed. A cupboard and drawers under the bench will usually look after the storage of other hand tools and any portable electric ones. Such cupboards should be carefully fitted out so that each item has its set place. This prevents everything from becoming jumbled up and having to sort through to find what is wanted. Portable power tools in particular have an in-built ability to get their leads tangled together at the slightest excuse.

There are several machines which the woodworker will find desirable, and in this respect his or her needs are possibly greater

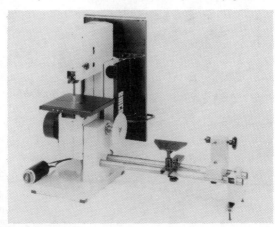

A combined band saw and lathe, the Emco Star 2000 is one of a wide range of machines from Emco for the home or small shop woodworker.

The Emco DB-6 woodworking lathe is a neat design and a good quality machine.

than that of a model engineer. A good bandsaw is one of the first items to be considered, as is a circular saw bench. A power planer and router make life easy, and a drilling machine is as essential almost to the woodworker as it is to the model engineer. Drilling machines can be fitted with mortising attachments very easily and these can increase accuracy as well as making light work of things. A woodworking lathe is also a desirable feature.

Over the years the manufacturers of woodworking equipment have been remarkably clever. A range of machines has been produced that will do a whole variety of jobs, which results in both a saving of space and expenditure. The best way to decide which

Myford Ltd. also make woodworking lathes. This one h as a bowl-turning faceplate outside the headstock and can be bought as a bench machine or on the smart cabinet shown.

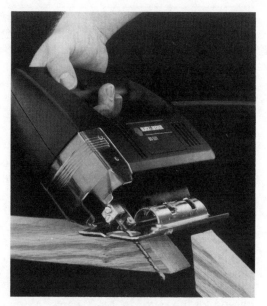

A powered jigsaw by Black and Decker has many uses out-side the woodworking shop proper.

of these might be the most suitable for one's needs is to visit a woodworking exhibition and see what is available. Portable power tools can also be obtained that will carry out a whole variety of jobs and so if there is not room for a permanent machine then the opportunity to work with power tools is still there.

Tool sharpening should be carried out with a wet stone grinder. This is a large grinding wheel which actually runs in water. The wheel travels at a much slower speed that the grinding wheels referred to in the chapter on grinding machines. Because of this and the continual flow of water over the stone there is little risk of the grinding particles flying round the workshop and so the grindstone can be sited near to other machines. Finishing of the sharpening process is carried out with an oilstone and these should be on wooden bases so that they can be rested on a bench when in use to aid accuracy.

It is not good practice to have woodworking and metal working facilities in the same workshop, but of course as space is invariably at a premium it may be a necessity. If so then try to keep the two types of machinery on separate sides of the building. Metal working will cause dirt and oil to spoil wood and woodworking will cause dust that is a nuisance to the metal worker. For this reason keep as much distance between the two types as possible.

15   AROUND THE WORKSHOPS

Throughout this book I have endeavoured to show how other people have utilised their space and facilities to create their own workshops by including photographs that show what others have done, to illustrate points I am trying to make. Everyone is an individual and has his or her own individual problems and this applies as much to setting up a workshop as it does to anything else in life. Each has particular needs and each a particular situation; marry the two and we get a vast permutation of possibilities. Mr A wants to build clocks and has a massive double garage for the purpose. Mr B wants to build 7¼ in. gauge model locomotives and only has a small garden shed, shared with the

The interior of Ralph Ley's workshop showing a quart in a pint pot. Notice how everything is laid out neatly and is easy to get at. Just visible behind the band saw is the drawing board. The lighting for this is provided by an illuminated magnifying glass which is an aid to accuracy.

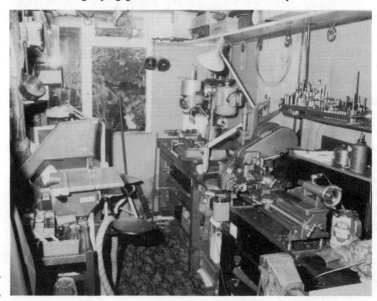

lawnmower etc. Mr C may want to make model boats and has to work in the loft, where he has to climb up and down with delicate models, and so it goes on.

Of course the ideal arrangement would be for Mr B building his large locomotives to swap with Mr A and Mr C could probably use the facilities of Mr B. What I am getting at is that there is rarely an ideal situation and we have to make the most of what we have. The following photographs will I hope show how well others have coped with the adaptation of various premises or managed to change what premises they have in order to get the best they can for their modelling.

Ralph Ley

Ralph builds model locomotives and traction engines as well as making various other models such as ploughs etc. Last time I saw him he was busy making a scale trestle bridge for five inch gauge track which was fully portable, as it could be taken to pieces in a matter of minutes. He works in an old conservatory attached to the house and the end of which is still used by his wife for raising plants. The result is he probably has the finest view of anyone I know when he looks out of his workshop.

It is a very small workshop and has everything packed into it. He has gone to a great deal of trouble over storage and made numerous drawers specifically to hold particular tools etc. with the result that he can immediately lay his hands on anything he wants. He has a small home-made Dore-Westbury milling machine and a Myford Speed 10 lathe. A bandsaw and a vertical drill-stand for a portable electric drill more or less complete the machinery side of things. His handworking bench contains a three inch vice. The workshop is well insulated and is lit with anglepoise lamps supplementing a fluorescent light. His was the only workshop that had a drawing board in it and this is tucked away to one side. It is a useful feature, particularly as Ralph likes to do his own thing. He can just leave what he happens to be doing and get on with some drawing as he wishes.

Dunstan Holt (*not illustrated*)

Dunstan has what is probably the most unusual workshop I have ever seen as far as construction is concerned. It is a small square building with a flat roof made entirely from concrete. The windows in it are small and high up and yet because of the way they are constructed give quite lot of light. It also means that light is coming in at a point where normally there would be walling that would not

Opposite, the neat layout of Bob Moore's workshop. Note the files stored in racks at the back of the handworking bench and the general absence of clutter. Above, Bob at one of the lathes. Metal can be seen stored in roof.

be used for any other purpose, while the inside of the walls can be used for storing material, tools etc.

Inside Dunstan has built his bench, also of concrete, and this is used both for working on and mounting the lathe. If one has the ability to get it perfectly smooth (as has Duncan) the material is ideal as it will not warp. The workshop has an overhead shaft for operating machinery, although the lathe, a Myford Super 7, has its own drive motor. An interesting feature was Dunstan's method of storing square lathe tools near the lathe in a little home-made rack. His grindstone occupies an entirely different building in an effort to keep grinding dust away from the machinery. The whole of the interior is painted white, which reflects the light and makes the workshop appear much larger than it really is.

Bob Moore
Bob works now professionally as a model engineer. He has managed to find himself quite a large building to act as a workshop and there is a Myford ML 7 lathe in it as well as quite a bit of heavy machinery, purchased second-hand. Metal is stored in the roof and stands have been built on which to keep models whilst work is being carried out on them. No matter when one visits there is always a calm air about the place, created by the

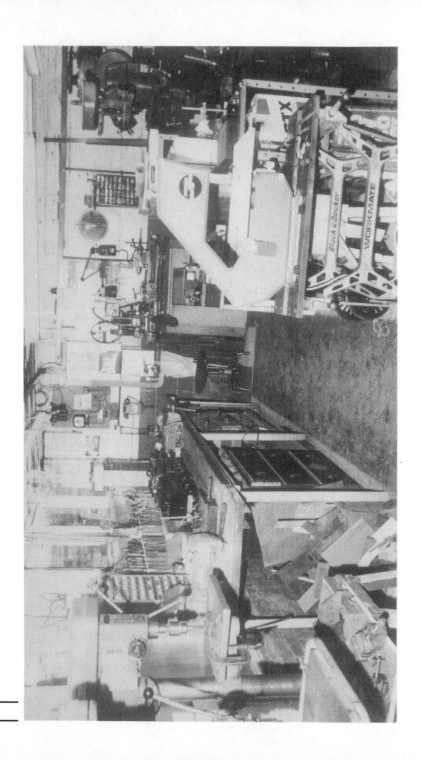

tidy way in which it is kept. This in itself leads to efficiency when working. Everything is readily available for use and there is no searching through to find tools etc. when required.

Lighting is entirely by means of fluorescent lights but they are strategically placed to give the best results at the machines which they illuminate. A row of windows provide a considerable amount of natural light. As one would expect from a professional modeller, there are useful items such as a big power saw and some large milling machines and lathes. However, a small bandsaw of the type illustrated in this book does quite a lot of work and is mounted on a Black and Decker Workmate.

Ted Jolliffe
Ted is the current editor of *Model Engineer* and his workshop is very much shared by his young son, who is a keen model engineer as well. The workshop is situated in a garage and has been well insulated and well stocked. It has been painted white to reflect light and to provide good illumination and this it certainly does very well. There are no windows at all and so all light is artificial and is from fluorescent lighting supplemented with anglepoise lamps.

Opposite, a view of the Bob Moore workshop from the door. Below, with a fairly large turnover of models organisation is necessary. The 5in. gauge Hunslet is on a specially prepared stand which makes it simple to move.

The workshop contains a large milling machine and a smaller one by Sigma Jones, both bought second-hand. There is a Zyto lathe, a make which alas is no longer produced. A small bench-mounted Kennedy hacksaw takes the hard work out of cutting metal bars and a bandsaw helps when cutting shapes from wood or metal. An unusual machine is a hand shaper. At one time these were very popular but these days are rarely seen and yet the finish that can be obtained on metal with one is quite superb. It apparently receives a lot of use. (*See also pages 21, 48 and 101*).

Bernie Buckland
Bernie likes making clocks. It has not always been thus and he has made stationary engines and locomotives in the past. He has a fairly large workshop in what I am sure he will not mind me saying is possibly the most unlikely looking garden shed that I have ever seen. The outside completely goes against all advice given in his book, but once inside the place is warm and cosy and is possibly as well insulated as any workshop I have ever seen. Over the years Bernie has collected a great deal of equipment and it is all stored neatly in the workshop.

He has a Myford lathe which has an extended bed as well as being raised over the mandrel and tailstock. He also has a

The grinder in Ted Jolliffe's workshop is kept well away from the machine tools; the nearest is the bench-mounted power hacksaw.

Another view of Ted's workshop: note sealed garage door. The bench-mounted Sigma Jones mill is unusual. Metal is stored under hacksaw.

watchmaker's lathe and a bench that is covered with green baize and kept specially clean for his clockmaking. Although Bernie is a clockmaker he is also a club man and does quite a bit of heavier work for the club when such things are required. Lighting is provided mainly by anglepoise type lamps situated where they are needed. Heating is by night storage heaters, Bernie having apparently tried all other types of heating without any real success. (*See page 50*)

Tony Challan
Tony Challan has a workshop which was built on to the rear of his garage. This is a popular place for a workshop as it gives one a self-contained building as well as the chance to use the garage if extra space is required. The workshop is built of building blocks.

It contains a Myford Super 7 lathe mounted on a home-made stand with shelving underneath to hold all the lathe accessories. This is a departure from the way most people work. The usual practice is to store the lathe accessories on shelving above the lathe. Tony, however, prefers to do it this way and it works well for him. The milling machine is set at a slight angle to allow room for work to be put on the milling table. One thing that is particularly noticeable is the very heavy worktops on the benches. Storage is in small plastic drawer units and other slightly larger drawers

Setting the milling machine at an angle makes it more accessible, as in this small end-of-garage workshop.

Below, Tony Challan puts his electrical sockets up high to avoid loose trailing wires. Note drill storage close to drill but high enough to avoid swarf. See also p.57.

under benches. The shelving is raised right up to ceiling height. Metal in short lengths is stored in a rack with squared off partitions and is similar to the idea of plastic guttering. Electrical sockets are placed quite high on the walls so that the danger of accident with trailing leads is avoided.

FINALLY A TALE OF A WORKSHOP AND WHAT CAN BE ACHIEVED WITH ENOUGH DETERMINATION

John Wilks
It is probable that one would never find another character such as John. A professional musician who was at one stage very famous in the music world, he has had a lifelong love affair with railways and particularly locomotives. His early modelling took the form of cardboard models of locomotives, this at that stage being the only means of modelling available to him. In 1962 he made up his mind that he would build a live steam model. The course John took is one that I would definitely not advise for the average person taking up the hobby. John, however, is definitely not average. He decided that he would build a five inch gauge model of a Great Western King class locomotive.

He managed to obtain a Myford ML 7 lathe and a ¼ inch drilling machine of doubtful parentage. His bench at that time was one half of the kitchen table. The other half was still used for food preparation. So with absolutely no engineering knowledge at all he started constructing the model. He freely admits to being grateful to several model engineers who have offered him advice over the years. The King started from a commercial design but soon became a scale model being constructed from works drawings. After a time he managed to find a bench, even if it was inclined to collapse if hacksawing was carried out too vigorously! In spite of this he finished a model that is really of exhibition standard as well as being a working locomotive with a great deal of power.

In 1965 he decided to make a model of an L.M.S. Coronation Pacific, again in five inch gauge. He then had a small workshop. Works plans were again obtained and a start made from those plans. No commercial castings were available and most of the locomotive was fabricated from solid metal. For example, the cylinders are cut from mild steel blocks, the bores of both cylinders and valves being lined. After four years he had to abandon all model engineering as work took him away and

John Wilks at work on one of his massive lathes. Adjacent shelves make stowage of accessories convenient to relative machine.

prevented further construction. The locomotive was finished some years later, again to the same very high standard both as regards looks and hauling power.

In the meantime the bug had really bitten, and as the result of a friendship with someone owning a 10¼ inch gauge railway he decided to build a locomotive to run on that gauge. Never one to shirk a challenge, he decided that it would be a massive American Niagara. A workshop was obtained, an old barn of a place, and some second-hand machinery invested in. Because of the massive heavy work he was about to undertake the machinery had to be very large too. It includes a couple of Colchester lathes, a Herbert vertical miller, large metal rollers, bandsaw, press and surface grinder.

A start was made. There was of course to be no lifting the locomotive on and off the bench. It will weigh several tons when finished, and a system of rail on rollers was devised as a stand. A hoist was also installed. The locomotive is now well on the way and very impressive it looks too. To tell all the dodges John has got up to make it would fill a book, and perhaps if we are lucky he will write one when it is finished. If he is not too busy making locomotives . . .

A very wise decision was to build both locomotive and tender together. How easy it would have been to have built just the locomotive and then later to have started the tender, which would then have been nothing more than a chore. Something that John has done to aid the construction is to have a lot of castings made. He insists only on very high quality from the foundries with which he deals, and most are lost wax. As a result of this he has become quite an expert on pattern and die making and the standard is such that it could easily have come from a professional firm.

Just for good measure he has purchased the chassis of an East African narrow gauge locomotive in 10¼ inch gauge, a massive 3 foot gauge 2-8-4 on which he has also done some work and which will no doubt follow the Niagara as soon as there is time. Perhaps what John is doing is not true model engineering and should be classed as light engineering. Make no mistake, though, John is model-making, whatever the size. Certainly it is not for most of us, but then we are not like John. I think that his efforts show what can be achieved if you put your mind to things. What a lovely success story it is, and seeing John, who has now retired, in his workshop is to see a very contented man.

INDEX

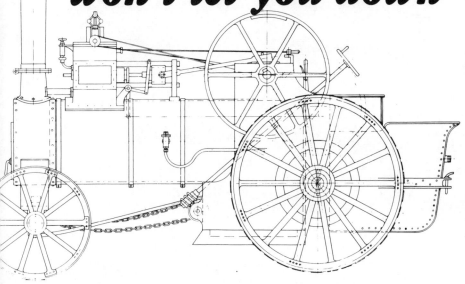